AF392007

Psithurism

Anthology by Realm of Poems

First published in 2020 by

Becomeshakespeare.com

One Point Six Technologies Pvt Ltd.
119-123, 1st Floor, Building J2, B - Wing,
WadalaTruck Terminal, Wadala East, Mumbai,
Maharashtra, India, 400022.
T: +91 8080226699

ISBN - 978-93-90266-30-2

DEDICATION

A home is known by its occupants. A poetic platform is worth its mentors, members and participants.

The group "Realm of Poems" was founded in the year 2019, and has since carved a place for itself in grooming budding writers and helping old hands in honing their skill further. This group is founded and administered by Mr Biraj Valia ably assisted by Ms Nirupama Jram. Both of them are blessed and inspired by poetic creativity thus they maintain this platform vibrant, active and at its creative best. This is also mentionable that the idea of this anthology was mooted & mentored by Mr Biraj Valia. This anthology is dedicated to group "Realm of Poems" This is dedicated to the rock solid member fraternity and not to forget the participants who made this process see the light of the day.

ACKNOWLEDGMENTS

The Team:
Mr Kumar Ramesh | Ms Jigna Mehta | Ms Prerna Anmol | Ms Nirupama Jram | Mr Biraj Valia

The acknowledgement is due to Mr Biraj Valia for mooting the idea of this anthology and putting all his weight and might to see it succeed.

The acknowledgement is also due to the dedicated and committed members of the group "Realm of Poems" for their consistent presence and participation in various poetic literary creative ventures that it undertakes from time to time.

The participants who have decorated the galaxy of this anthology are the sparkle of the day and their contributions is acknowledged with deep sense of gratitude and belongingness. Last but not the least, the team of die hard enthusiasts who relentlessly strived to put this anthology in the shape we find it now, are the binding cord of different pages of this humble start.

THE POETS

PREFACE

*Realm of Poems is a family of poets on Facebook,
sharing and reviewing each other's poems.*

Daily writing prompts by different members encouraged
everyone to keep writing new poems. Free verse, rhyming
couplets and more complex poetry forms, all blooming
beautifully. We have poets from all over the globe, here there
are no boundaries of geography, age or religion. All are bonded
together with words, words of emotions, words of love, words
of pain. Words flow freely like wind or like waves of an ocean,
like wildflowers, like a free flowing river. For our beautiful
family, it was only imperative to have our book published
for each of us to remember and cherish for life. We have
intentionally not followed any particular theme for the writers.
Readers would love the myriad poems in this book, which
would take one on a voyage of surprises. Each page you turn
will have intriguing poetry having a unique style and theme. All
are welcome to be part of our family by joining our Realm of
Poems group on Facebook.

Aafiya Siddiqui

Aafiya is a girl from India. She had worked as a researcher and lecturer in the field of Applied Sciences. Currently she works as a freelance content writer in the health and fitness domain.
In her leisure time, she enjoys penning down her thoughts and endeavours to paint the canvas of life through its shades of black and white with her poetic expressions.i

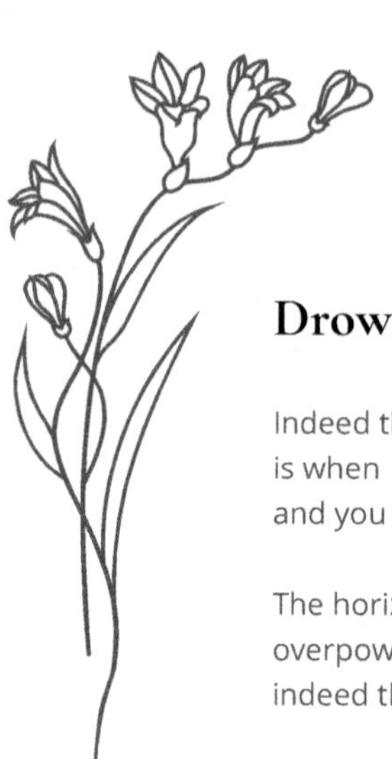

Drowning

Indeed the worst kind of feeling
is when you're stuck in the blues
and you know you are sinking

The horizons of hope are diminishing
overpowered by the darker hues
indeed the worst kind of feeling

As the night of fear is suffusing
you try to break the cues
and you know you are sinking

The dreams of shore are still appealing
but deserted heart is stranded in rues
indeed the worst kind of feeling

Watching helplessly as the sun is drowning
with deafening silence taking a cruise
and you know you are sinking

How can you give up fighting
how can you look for excuse
indeed the worst kind of feeling
and you know you are sinking
©aafiya_21

Words

"I chew my words silently
Why should I waste them on
A heartless like you?
Who choses to ignore them,
To whom they are of no value"
While I was busy contemplating
I found him smiling
As if he knew,
what I was going through
Perhaps he mastered the art
of reading the eyes too
"Words are a magic wand
For the poetic wizards,
They act like a bridge between
The hearts that differed
But for the hearts that
Beat in choral symphony
Words are better left unsaid."
There on the seer spoke boldly
©aafiya_21

Adnan Shafi

Young Adnan Shafi, (23) was born and brought up in a middle class educated Bhat family, which belongs to Chandrigam in Tral area of Kashmir valley. He is a poet, writer, columnist, translator, short story writer, reviewer, blogger, motivational speaker, ghazal-writer and editor.
Coauthor of many anthologies, Author at DESTINY POETS UK.
He has been internationally published and won poetry awards from numerous publications.
His poetry book "TEARS FALL IN MY HEART' depicts sorrows and vicissitudes of life. There are various hues in his poems ranging from love to loneliness and despair. Besides, his poetry is replete with the simplicity of thought and language. Some of the poems are autobiographical in nature which relate to his own life's vows.

Poetry

I read poetry for pleasure
An ongoing treasure.

I read it to love...
It is an imminent trove

I read it to find..........
What is on your mind

It gives consoling to my soul
When taken it from another goal
©Adnan Shafi

Not fairest in my art

Ay, Not fairest in my art,
ay, not owning the decent
well-made clothes,
behind the foundation,
hiding acne,
ay, not having a perfect
portrait of a countenance,
and an ideal figure; love, my flaw,
ay,not being fair enough for it as
time has ravaged me and offered
grief.
©Adnan Shafi

Akpodiogaga Benedicta Oghenetega

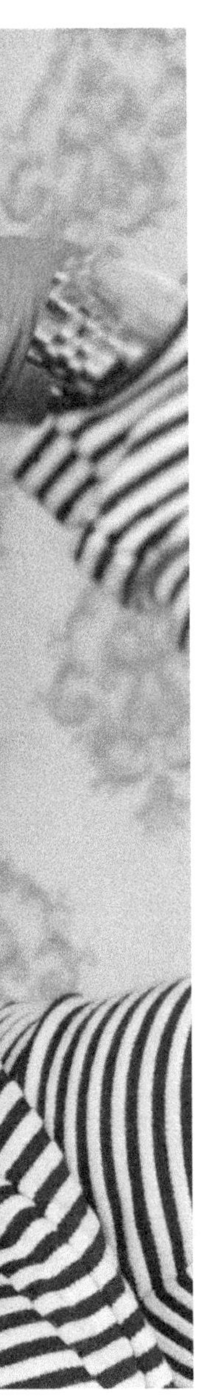

Akpodiogaga Benedicta Oghenetega, known by her pen name as Tega Benny, was born on 6th October, in the city of Lagos Nigeria, to a family of seven siblings of Mr Francis and Mrs Mary Akpodiogaga. She had a background education at Ajeromi primary school, St. Saviors High School and an alma mater of the University of Benin, Benin City, Edo State Nigeria, with a BSc in Sociology and Anthropology.

She is business manager with a career pursuit in the fashion and beauty industry. She is an avid lover of God and a firm believer in empathetic living, which is reflected in her writings, with a fervor of subtlety and esthetic reflections, she conveys emotions in varying poetry forms. She is very passionate about writing and has a penchant for books, travelling, music, movies and meditative cerebration. Amenable to learning, exploring and adventure.

Past, present... future

A day old epoch of spring
Stood at the end of my tree
On broken branches
Were blooms I never could pick again
Desirous as they are
Only full of carnivorous sweetness
Watching them wither
Was the very test
Losing taste of each bite to winter years
Parched against the soil
Vulnerable bark faced the weather
Albeit erect on bland root
Deciduous in desedimentation
Transiting a new orientation
Soaking in the rain of gratification
Watered in the persistence to wax
Sharing the love of the sun
As another spring arrives
Smelling of buds I have chosen to groom
Alas uncertain of how many will remain in
autumn
Perchance these greens will relapse to
sorrel crimps
And I will falter to hold them together
But I trust I will be safe as I wander
Journeying throughout different border
As I live out the script of my maker
©tega_benny

Warrior of light

Shining through the bleak of night
Standing on the pointedness of truth
Excavating eyes of enervating gloom
Come fort, take shelter from the release of my
loom

The clarion call of liberation champions my
soul
Armed and ready to conquer weeping coals
Wielding a weapon in an ear
I will bield a way for your fears

Reigning on the darkness of plundered honor
For the battle of justice, I heave the cross of
valor
Bounded by the sworn oath to share a glow
I will shield you in love against transgressor
blow

Summoning the artillery of will to power
Courage hope peace some love, my soldiers
and flag bearer
Prepared to outshine chiaroscuro tyranny
Anointed to beam the lantern of epiphany

Arise from the flattery of squalor
Behold the crest of comfort on my armor
Vanquishing evils in cold depths of steel
I will sharpen the blades of prayer for the
miracle of my light to heal..
©tega_benny

Ankita Baheti

Ankita Baheti was born on 15 September 1986 at Gandhinagar. She is B.E.(Hons.) in electronics n communication field and was a meritorious student throughout her life. She worked as Assistant professor in engineering college, then after marriage she worked as technical content developer in a company in Gurugram. Then she shifted to Qatar and worked as freelancer. She had inclination towards poetry and article writing right from her childhood. She generally likes to write about nature, feminism, social issues etc. Currently she is a full time mother, taking tuitions and trying to contribute to society through her strong, message bearing poems and articles

Poetry

When words
Face each other
In rhymed or unrhymed
Lines to contrive
Thaumaturgic
With some
Exquisite
Fascinating Style
Like ode, ballad, sonnet,
Haiku, limerick, quatrain,
Rime, rune or free verse
Or any...

When they nudge
Reader's heart, mind
And make amore to soul,
Then that composition
Effectuate its purpose,
Fetching Zephyr
Of elation and comfort.
©_bahetiankita

Speak up

Speak up, when you like something,
Your appreciation can make someone's day.

Speak up, when you feel its wrong,
Your voice can give others, strength to fight.

Speak up, when you are sad,
Your worries can be solved with others advise.

Speak up, when you are in doubt,
Your conversation can clear misunderstanding.

Speak up, when you are upset with something,
Problems may get solution with different
perspective.

Speak up, when you feel hurted,
Your experience can save someone.

Speak up, when you don't like something,
Your words can help someone improvise.

Speak up, when you are happy,
As passing on happiness is the best way to be
happy.

Whatever happens in life, Don't hide,
Don't keep mum, don't lock yourself,
Just Speak up, as this the beautiful gift we
have!!
©_bahetiankita

Ann Jarmolowicz

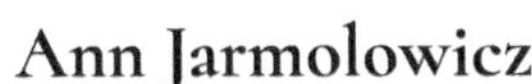

Ann Jarmolowicz has published 2 poetry books in the last 2 years 'The Naked Soul" and Seasons of the Soul' and is currently working on a third book. Her books are circulating in 14 countries and she has an international following on her Facebook poetry page : www.facebook.com/ajthenakedsoul
Her first published poem was featured in an anthology 'Mad Like Us 2018' which was selected for publication from an international poetry competition on the theme of mental health.
She has written poetry for many years and has travelled extensively which is reflected in some of her work. A former teacher of modern languages and now retired she continues to indulge in her passion for travelling and immerse herself into the world of wordy things

Strange New World

Strange New World, brave we need to be.
Endure and tolerate in adversity.
Our lives as we know it are under threat,
New vocabulary learned, new stringent
measures set.
Social distancing now the new norm in force.
"Stay at home!" or regret , be filled with
remorse.
Never before has technology been such a
useful tool,
Streaming 'stay at home activities' to adhere
to the rule.
Essential travel only or shopping for basics,
Strange New World all of us in "The New
Matrix."
Shutdown, lockdown on human behaviours,
Frontliners, keyworkers becoming our
saviours.
A neighbourly love full of compassion,
Reaching out to the vulnerable in such a
friendly fashion.
Mother Nature is healing in all of this mess,
Butterflies, bees, birds in morning chorus.
Canals turning blue, dolphins returning,
Animals freely in city streets roaming.
Clearer skies from a drop in pollution.
Take only what is needed, a new resolution?
When all of this is over and the pandemic
stops winning.
Let's hope humans learn of a new beginning!
©ajthenakedsoul

Grief

She sits quietly in the wings.
One can only respect what she brings.
As the drama unfolds on the stage,
Unprompted, she appears with all her rage.
She bites with an angry tongue,
At those who have done no wrong.
Her pain is heavy on the heart,
Feels like it is ripping apart.
From nowhere the tears begin to flow,
At any moment, difficult to know.
She appears so unexpectedly,
Maybe a fleeting memory.
A song, a smell, an image, a taste,
She comes and goes, she has no haste.
Try not to cage her, just let her breathe,
She needs to be released from those who grieve.
Beneath all her pain and teary eyes,
Is where all of her love lies.
©ajthenakedsoul

Anupam Mishra

Anupam Mishra, a language trainer by profession from Mumbai, who loves the world of the words, sharing the emotions and life experiences using the same. She belongs to the land of Maa Janaki, Sitamarhi in Bihar. She has done her graduation in Education and Post Graduation in English Literature from IGNOU. She has been in the profession of teaching for ten years. She has been writing poems, stories and anecdotes since she was in 7th and chooses to write in almost every form and style.

A Story

It's no more different from any other story,
Where the protagonist longs for the glory,
Even in the adversities, eagers to be merry,
Here I'm to narrate the history from her
diary.

The first page she had left blank in confusion
Thinking whether to disclose or hide her
derision,
Finally took the decision to conceal but
mention
As it would have created more pain than
relaxation.

She started to state the rest with sheer
conviction
Gathering every readers' and listeners'
attention.
'A Lost Identity' was at the top as her
introduction
From where she starts to share her
perception.

"I believed I was the best, blessed with
everything
That's required for an Indian girl for a
luxurious living
Being the eldest I have got almost all the
privilege
In the joint family with some sort of royal
heritage.

Aspiring to be at the pinnacle through all
the obstacles
I considered that all my dreams will become
real
As I contemplated myself as a god gifted
child special
Mixing every reality with what actually was
virtual.

Neither my parents nor teachers could
tame me
And I emerged out as a revolutionary
individual
Seeking spiritualism in various sort of
animals
I lost faith in the Almighty and His beloved
humans.

It was not just because of any particular
situation
But the cause was nothing but lack of
motivation
That even provoked me to reach for the
salvation
Without even fulfilling what was in my
authorization.

How indigent I had been that I couldn't even
see
Or listen to the reality that was so close to
me!
With the help of the light burnt with the
wisdom free
I started to live with strength, knowledge
and dignity.

Today I can claim with the dissolved

agitation
Along with my inner self filled with
consideration,
Anyone like me can change the prepared
presentation
With a ray of hope enlightened with internal
inspiration."

Though I've seen her growing into a
matured one
From the naive, ignorant girl to an ideal
woman,
I know very well that there's still a lot
hidden
Even from her own self, what's lying within.
©Anupam Mishra

My Moon

I sat in stillness all alone
One night under the sky
When all slept except the moon
Who greeted me with eternal smile
In silence we converse for a while
And then bid each other bye.

Zealously to meet him I came out
After a long day on the other night
But he was nowhere in the heaven
Though the stars were scattered there.
I woefully missed his presence
As I'd to say something in his agile ear.

I thought he too had ditched me
Like the other important ones in my life
So in annoyance I sat in the dark.
To my astonishment he came back
With the same smile he materialized
Provoking me to forget what's passed.

I asked, "Where have you been?"
He just smiled saying nothing
Silently training me to get habituated
With whatever has been happening.
Now I could see him grow and disappear
With the same love and warmth forever.
©Anupam Mishra

Arti Verma

Arti Verma, a resident of USA. She has always been attracted by poems. She loves reading poetry in English , Hindi and Urdu. She is an Human Resource professional by career. She also likes gardening and deep conversations. Fabric painting is a newly acquired interest of her.
Women's issues are very close to her heart and she finds herself gravitating towards them in life and in her writings.

50% Chance of Shower

Days will pass and turn into years
But I will remember you without any cares
Before you morphed in front of me
Into a different person I saw you
Now with every layer I see a bit of you
Was it a bit I missed or you grew?
Can one person be two people
Or is it just life's lessons nimble?
As I watch trying to understand
The hot and cold, the warm and distant
Things are changed not so pristine
But affections go deep and roots are strong
So maybe there will be a new sprout after
all
A new binding which is nothing like old
helping me to accept the new mould
For nothing remains as it was ever
So maybe I need to erase the forever
And take it everyday as it comes,
watch each new sprout with interest
For haven't I loved and unloved you more
times than I remember?
So I will just keep space for the new you
©Arti Verma

Rape Of A Girl

I never got the chance to see the world,
beyond my home there are wonders I am
told .
Long before I was born the society wished
me unborn,
Coming into the world I was always a bit
lorn.
Running out and staying out the boys could
do,
Things I loved I wanted to do
Advised to be quiet and coy was I .
" Doesn't she look pretty? "was the most I
came by.
I wanted to climb trees and soar in the
clouds,
But they had already started putting me in
shrouds.
"Stay at home, cook and clean,
World to girls going out is so mean".
Rape was a weapon shown not a word,
A constant threat in which my life was mold.
My aspirations choked and my desires
killed,
My earth was left barren and never tilled .
" Don't go there... Don't do that
The wolf man shall come and it will be the
end "
I was the doll who was petted and admired,
But when I wanted to fly everyone got tired.
A doting daughter, wife and mother,
That was my life and none another.

I stayed on the path and stayed near home,
I stayed in at night and didn't leave my
dome.
But the wolf man came for me still...
It plucked me from my yard
And had its fill.
As I lay dying in my last breath
How I wished I had learnt to fly before my
death
O why did you not let me fly?
©Arti Verma

Even after getting chased by zephyr

this silly heart of mine is chasing the tune of

psithurism,isolated by feel of mine it's note offers me tunes to

fill my realm of poem

© njram6

Ayo Gutierrez

Ayo Gutierrez pens her art in the Philippines. She is a professional speaker and a TV personality. Some of the books she authored and co-authored are Bards from the Far East (haiku collection). Yearnings, Chasing Zephyrs, Evocare (tanka collection), Amalgam, and the Amazon
bestseller Almost is the Same as Never. She is also the owner of GMGA Publishing, having published more than 50 authors worldwide.
Haiku and Tanka are her favorite poetry forms to write.
Reading her words is indulging the soothing satisfaction of crackling fire; hot chocolate running down your throat in the unfolding of her journey she leads— rich, earthy, and sure

Musings of a Canvas

I watch your dishevelled stance
glazed eyes burning—
lost in raging vagaries
of cataclysmic wars
shadows eclipse your eyes
as your visions swirl—
ever-changing like the seasons
anticipation ...
trepidation ...
how I ache for your release
not once
have you touched me...
yet completely
you consume me
In a frenzied
loving flash—
your brush
meets my nakedness
suddenly I swim
awash in a roiling sea
of breathless turbulent colours
but joyously I now suffocate
in the winds of your tempest
till naked no longer ....
in stillness
at last
I revel
under the scrutinous gaze
of raging fans and critics
yet their opinions matter not—
before you

I was void ....
but you find beauty lurking

where others fail to find it
and though I may gather dust ...
from time to lonely time
your soul and touch transformed me
and I am yours to paint
again, and again—
and again
©Ayo Gutierrez

Contretemps

...Many break the mirror that
reminds them of their ugliness
But you keep yours, stained and scarred
...You revel in villainy to ascertain yourself
an infamous note of notoriety
...in so much
that your distinction becomes your defect
.... Your arguments are too loud that they
degenerate into bubbles.
...Many are famished; they heed only to fill
their stomachs,
albeit the worst of rubbish.

—Fools once, fools a hundred times—

...Bracelets of counterfeit sapphires dangle
(insouciantly) from their wrists
...Parlor maids polishing coffin lids

of them dead— disdainful and dead

—You are no different—

...The night has not left us; you are still
standing amidst shadows—petrified to
continue
descending

....and this is not the poem where you
welcome the uncertainty of the outcome.

'Tis not so.

.... You must make amends:
... to separate your soul from its lineaments.
...to be exact in an era of approximation.
...to tenderize the armor that your
beleaguered flesh has become.
...Make amends, I say
Until all contradicting hearts are won.
©Ayo Gutierrez

Those feelings are deep riddle Searching answers

betwixt invisible past Psithurism of hope making a

way Traversed a long path unknowingly My dream

a canopied projection.

© njram6

Biraj Valia

Biraj Valia an entrepreneur and an electronic engineer. Working as the CTO at Beegees India, he often travels across the country for work. It was during these long business trips that he started writing travelogues.
Only a couple of years back he was drawn to writing poems. Learning new forms of poetry, experimenting with rhyme schemes and syllables intrigued him. Simplicity with an easy flow of expression gives his poems a unique style. His writings comprise aesthetic zeal and exuberance.

Tango of Life
Trenta-Sei Poem Form

Two souls moving in rhythm
Her head held back with pride
Her steps in his passion exalt him
With her arm anchored in his stride
Holding her close with love so rife
Fascinating dance of intimate life
Her head held back with pride
Burgundy gown swaying in glee
As he carries her in a swirl ride
Fascinating moments of nestle
Joy illuminated darkness of life
Lost in music of violin and fife
Her steps in his passion exalt him
Enthralled by her fragrance of lilac
Sweetness igniting fire within In him
Holding her high in the sky so black
Lilac love of purity embellishing sight
Dance of leader and follower so right
With her arm anchored in his stride
Striving to breathe free from his clutch
Her life so enclosed in the dark cried
Steps withdrawing from his touch
Each swirl of moment now so dizzy
Sound of music made her feel tizzy
Holding her close with love so rife
Left him with scars across his chest
Smell of lilac now like cloying knife
Shattered heart sprawled stressed
Every move to lift her spirit was in vain

Music of love faded from life so bane
Fascinating dance of intimate life
The game was to hold the other close
Sway in close and open embrace all life
Turns with trust and steps of love shows
Love is forever to cherish in life
Life is a tango and tango is life
©birajv

Moonless Night

Interlocking Rubaiyat Poetry Form

Romance midst moonless night
Beauty silken skin wrapped invite
Dazzling full moon visage shining
Fragrant night jasmine excite
Curls sway with zephyr beginning
Earings over her nape swinging
Pearls shining as rose petals curve
Inviting my fervour while grinning
Chimes of anklets as she swerves
Clinking bangles in alluring verve
The warmth of inglenook unfurls
Flaring we entwine to observe
A night with full moon visage turns
Housed in embrace so warm firms
Kisses of rose glistened with love
Redolence of adoration swirls
©birajv

Bishakha Moitra Prajapati

Born on 2nd May 1980, in a small town, Serampore, in the Hoogly district of West Bengal, Bishakha, is an artist (a writer and a painter) by passion. She completed her graduation in commerce and her post graduation in business administration with specialization in marketing and HR. After working in corporate sector for 10 years she chose to be a stay at home mom. Writing to her is penning down, expressing her, emotions, views, thoughts, feelings and opinions in a way that others can understand and feel the connect. Prior to this she has contributed to few other anthologies and some of her penned stories have also been published online. Bishakha uses "a gypsy soul" as a pen name as she thinks this is what she truly is, a wanderer at heart. You can read her writings and follow her page on instagram www.instagram.com/thoughtsofagypsysoul

Your Embrace

That warm clasp of your arms around,
Shielding me, protecting me
Like a shade from the burning sun
Sheltering me with your embrace
From the storm brewing outside
And also inside my heart and mind
The warmth, the care, the love
Which envelopes me, taking my breath
away
Making me forget all my longing and pain
Compelling me to lose myself, let myself
sway
In these perimeter of endearment and
intimacy
Making me believe everything else is
worthless
In amidst so much of chaos it gives me
Sense of peace, freedom and privacy
Melting all my worries and sorrow
Consuming me in that moment of passion
As if there is no tomorrow
As if there is no tomorrow
©agypsysoul

Speechless

You came like a whirlwind
And swept me off my feet

Before I knew you picked me up ,
Held me tight
Pronounced your love and
kissed me right
With the emotions so unexplainable
And the love so strange and senseless
I was left completely speechless

With love that crazy
You carried me away in land of dreams
I fell head over heels for you
Before I could understand
I was madly in love with you
The love gave me wings
I was flying high
I just wanted to be with you
For you I was even willing to die
I never knew I was capable of
This love which was so daring and fearless
I was again left completely speechless

Then suddenly it was over and done
Before I could comprehend
There was not a trace of you, none
You were gone like you were never there
I was left vulnerable and my soul bare
I fell down from the sky
Now in the bottom of deepest trench I lie
I am alive but you dig my grave
Neither did I wished nor anyone could save
Love which was so strong and reckless
Also was so fragile and hopeless
I was yet again left completely speechless
©agypsysoul

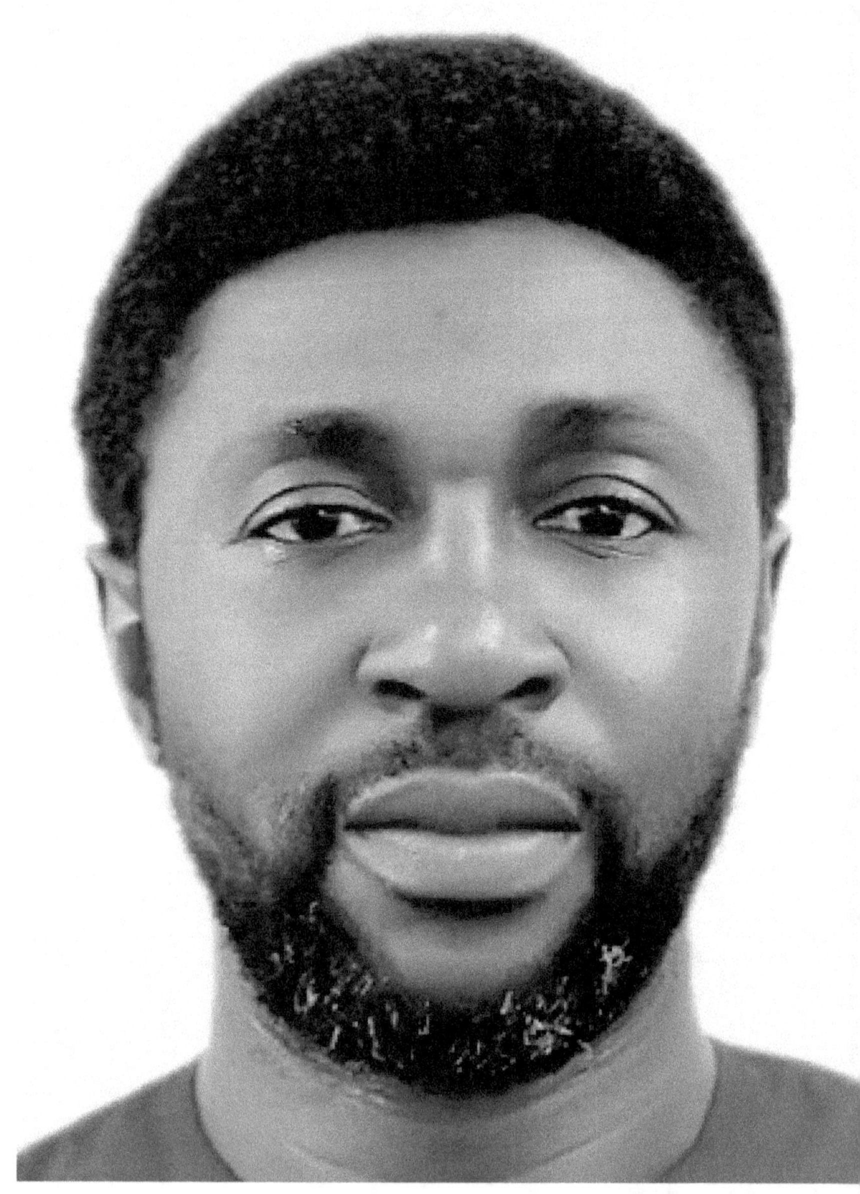

Francis Otole

Francis Otole is a Nigerian from the Middle Belt
region of Benue state. He is an avid reader and lover
of books. He is a poet of over six hundred (600)
poems to his credit with literary commendations
and awards. He is a member of numerous literary
groups with contributions. He is an educationalist, a
researcher, philanthropist and a pro-earth; lover of
nature and humanity.

Poetic inspiration

60

Nature's spree
Of being free
Brings the mind to glee.

Sometimes rue
Brings many hues
That paints life new.

Aimless logic
The basic magic
Of colorful music.

Psychic infiltration
By beauty's admiration
Sources of poetic inspiration.
©Francis Otole

Love's complex curve

It has come to my notice
None in love is a novice.
Even though love is blind,
It leads you right to find.

There are many proven facts
About passionate lovers acts.
Those whom love lead to find
Always act like they are blind.

I have seriously taken study
From different faculties body.
This delicate thing called love
Has a straight and complex curve.
©Francis Otole

Hari Prasad.S

Hari Prasad.S is an engineer by profession and likes
to write poetry on many emotions and is also an
amateur photographer.
He likes to express his thoughts through poetry and
his views through his photography.
He has hosted websites www.assortedemotions.
com for his poetry and 500px.com/shprd74 for his
photography.

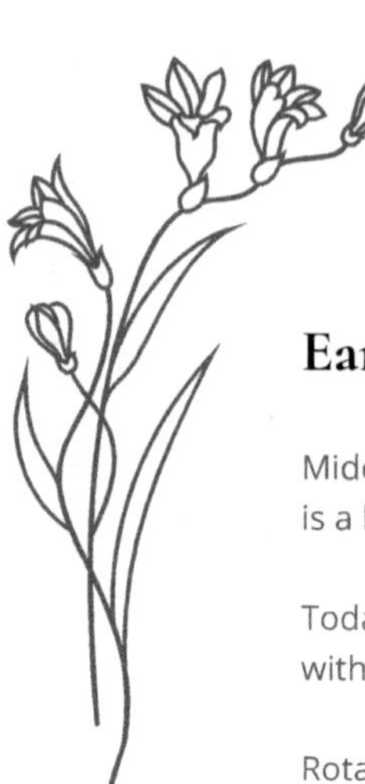

Earth song

Middle of wheel,
is a battle real.

Today I will play,
with just wet clay.

Rotating round and round,
I'll let symmetry surround.

With fingers gentle,
I'll press, push and pull.

Beautiful pot & vase,
surround my space.

My heart sings,
an accomplished song.

I've within found a meaning.
from the song, my earth has sung.

Think beyond you surround,
don't just merry go round.
©Hari Prasad.S

Concealed paradise

In my anchorless sleep,
I'm consciously dwelling deep.

Playing all night is a dreadful,
stale tale.

The oceans tide is ravaging my shore,
exposing my hidden abode.

The moon that was on crescent, has turned
full,
I keep praying him to remain dull.

His vision for me has blurred,
putting me in deep trouble.

Awaiting for dewdrops to fall '&' turn me to
a pearl,
I woke up once more, stuck within my shell.
©Hari Prasad.S

Jeanette D'Souza

Jeanette D'Souza born on 12th March 1967 in
Mumbai, Maharashtra has done her Bachelor in
Arts with Economics. She is full time home maker as
well as part time Art Teacher. She loves everything
connected to art, like gardening, cooking, music,
drawing, painting, collection of stamps, reading.
Jeanette has been in love with writing from the age
of eleven. She lives her life in slow motion, and hates
the fast paced life that is prevalent.

Pushing Daisies

A Seer could not read my palms or
forehead.
And foresee the hour I might be dead.

No Soothsayer, no Crystal balls, no Tarot
cards,
No Mystics, no Priest, no Witch craft.

No, none can tell when I'll be gone.
Yet I know.... I'll definitely be done.

No King, No beauty, No saint, No thug,
was ever able to hoodwink death's looming
hug.

So when it happens, and I can't tell you
time.
If you be there to lay me to rest in my
destined space.
Please, Please do not throw a slab over
mine.

I want not a tomb stone,
a symbol,
nor your engraved words of gold.
For, what purpose would it serve.
While I lived, I was never told.

Just put me down gently.
Wrapped...in linen.
Cover me softly with sod.

When I am heavily sleeping.
Let the vermin do their job.

Then, scatter the seeds.
I love so much.
No. No not the exotic kind.
Those simple, humble, generous &
forgiving.
Oooh! those lovely ladies.
Them field daisies.

I'll give to earth & soil my best.
That's how you'll know,
I don't want to rest.

Whenever you pass by,
turn your head my way.
Or maybe just your eye.

You'll delight in the splendour you see and...
Realize it was not just my thumb or my toe
that was green,
but all of me.
I was much more.

You'll then exclaim,
"There she is toiling again,
pleasing our souls......
'Pushing Daisies' ".
©Jeanette D'Souza

Complicated

My doe eyed princess
The first time I set eyes on you
My heart skipped a beat
But I knew right from the start
We were already treading different paths
Not letting you go...my only fault
As the grit stones on your path seemed
treacherous and savage
I thought I'd stay a while
till on your own
you could manage
but those precious minutes spent
led us to melt
I am sorry my dove
Did not expect you to fall in love
No 'secret' love had I kept
You were aware of 'her' when we met
I leave you as I found you...flawless
Knowing I had made you no promises
I've never done anything against your will
And my promise to wed 'her' I must fulfill
My parting message you must accept
Why! things happen the way they do....
God only knows best
©Jeanette D'Souza

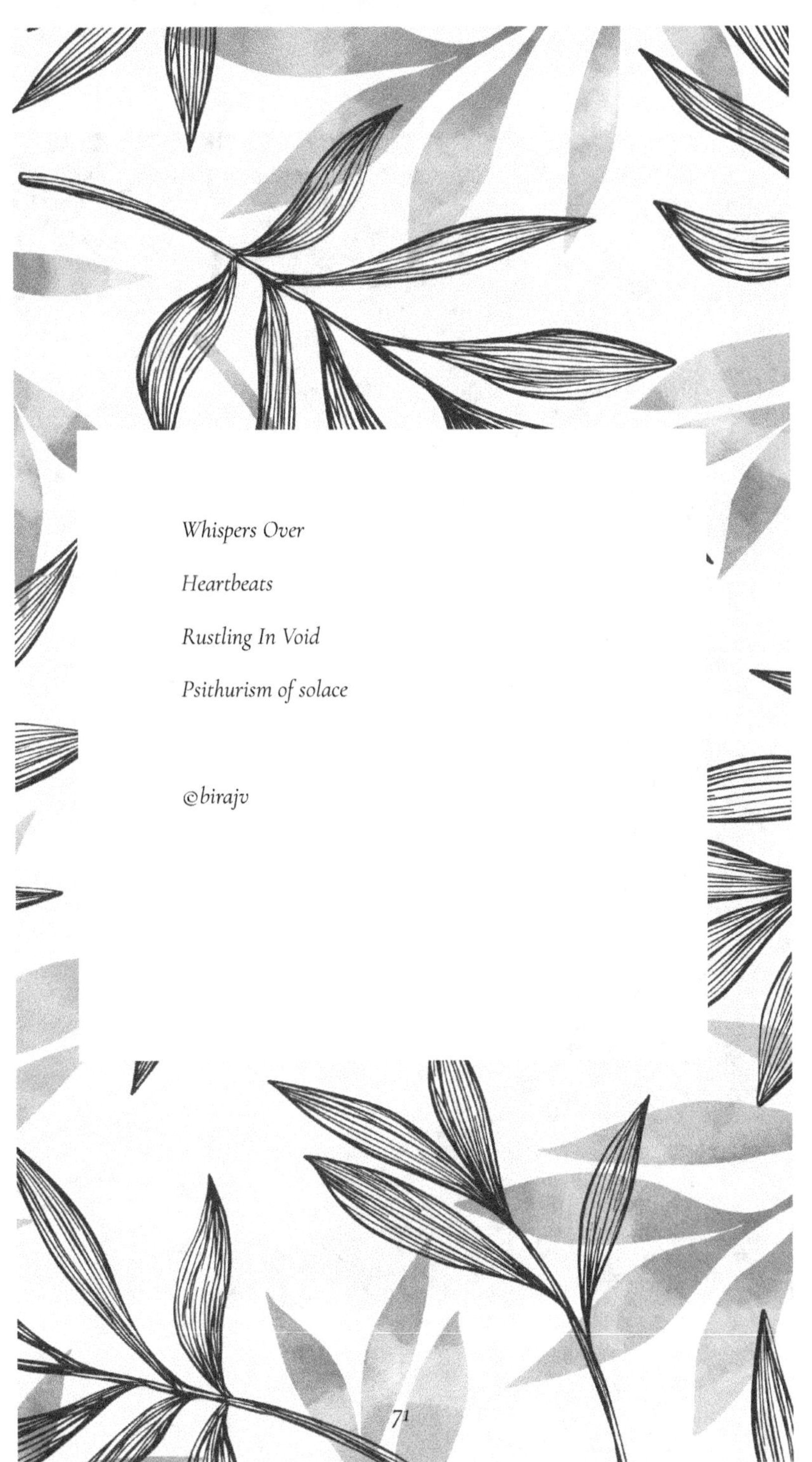

Whispers Over

Heartbeats

Rustling In Void

Psithurism of solace

@birajv

Jigna Mehta

Jigna Mehta belongs to Rajkot, Gujrat. She has completed her B.SC in Food and Nutrition. She is a dedicated housewife. She believes in the simplicity of life and carries her proudness in mundane works. Writing gives her glee and gratification and a defined direction to her life. She loves to prepare poems with the ingredients of celestial imagination, delicate emotions and sensitive feelings with the taste of appropriate selection of words on the flame of realistic scenario and serve with extra cheese of love and beauty. The aroma of her delicious recipes already make a presence in other anthologies too

Girls are always grey

These women are either black or white,
nah..nah dear you are mistaken,
as girls are always grey.

You think they smile and slay,
or consider thyself as their prey,
nah..nah dear you are mistaken,
as girls are always grey.

You always suspect them,
ever think about that what's the thing,
which mostly affect them?
Ohhhh...you are so smart,
spontaneous answers are,
they love the flattery or attention,
or true love and communication,
so thoughtful of you all,
but ever think about what they want?
ever think about that one word?
called "RESPECT",
anyways......,,
as girls are always grey.
©Jignaa

Never surrender

Never surrender to life or to death,
Neither to obstacles nor to fate,
Keep one thing in mind..........,
Repeat it over and over again,
Keep your head high ,
Either in bliss or in pain,
Everything will be at peace,
Everyone stays,
When you love yourself,
You will find more ways,
So......
My love,
Never surrender.
©Jignaa

Linda Rivas Bole

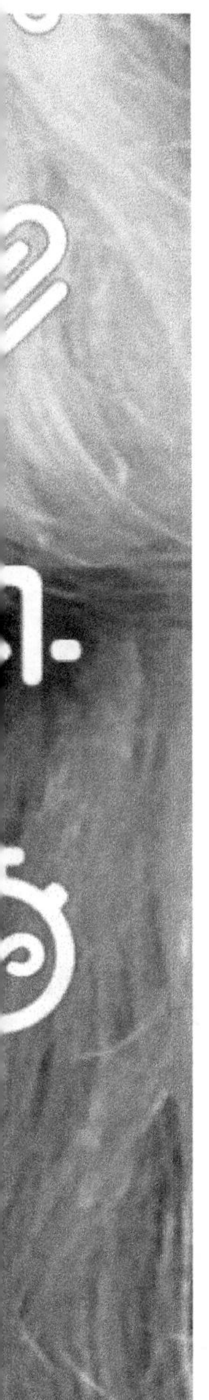

 Linda has been writing poetry since she learned
it existed. Words that put together helped others
feel emotions and find a path to their own field of
desire. As a college student she became interested in
different forms of poetry and wrote many different
types of poetry but settled into free form because of
the flow and non constricting value

My Last Memory of Home

the last memories
of home
leave me wistful
haunted and happy
Mom in the kitchen
baking cookies
while I watched
smells wafting
in clouds
around...surrounding
my existence
while weather emanated
summers past
Mom smiled that day
and acted
like she loved me
then...
I started on my journey
joining flows of life
when I was through
home was
gone and
life would never
be the
same
©Linda

The Music of the Wind
Pantoum Poetry Form

Have you ever heard the music of the wind
Did you ever see the beauty of the storm
The wind song makes opera sound
chagrined
It's wild and the savage do perform

Did you ever see the beauty of the storm
The lightening and the thunder are
untamed
It's wild and the savage do perform
View the beauty of it now unconstrained

The lightening and the thunder are
untamed
I watch it out the window mesmerized
View the beauty of it now unconstrained
The flashing and the forks might hurt your
eyes

I watch it out the window mesmerized
My heart smiles at the splendor of the night
The flashing and the forks might hurt your
eyes
The lightening makes the darkness shine so
bright

My heart smiles at the splendor of the night
The wind blows the rain against the trees
The lightening makes the darkness shine so
bright

The gale distorts the bushes with such ease

The wind blows the rain against the trees
Howls and whips and songs of wild life
The gale distorts the bushes with such ease
I listen to the mournful dirge stabbing like
a knife

Howls and whips and songs of wild life
The wind song makes opera sound
chagrined
I listen to the mournful dirge stabbing like
a knife
Have you ever heard the music of the wind
©Linda

On banks of dream's flowing stream

When drenched in those memories.

Rustle and whisper caress my soul,

Psithurism drums life in my arteries.

Soothes ruffled feather & consoles,

Cajoles me back to pleasant reveries.

@Kumar Ramesh

Mayank Dhar

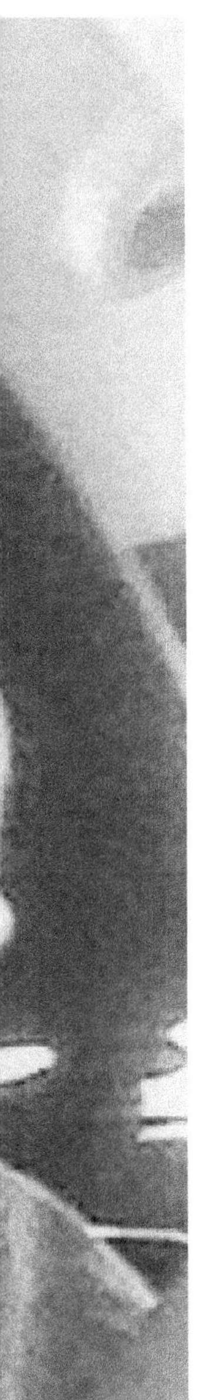

Born at Kangra, Himachal Pradesh on 25th April, Mayank Dhar is a content and communication consultant. He has gained his education from Gurugobind Singh Indraprastha University in Bachelors of Information systems and done Diploma in Journalism and mass communication from IGNOU. He began his career with a newspaper called PIONEER. He has worked extensively on many content development and communication projects with organisations such as Aurobindo Society. Mayank has written for many online platforms under the pen name "culpritwords". His writings highlight human feelings and social issues like child molestation, women empowerment etc. He is also an avid food blogger also and his writings can be followed and read on instagram at www.instagram.com/culpritwords

What is Love

84

Love is stroke of serendipity or melancholy
It can't be that easy to decide
Because gone-bys vouch for former
Telling, nothing could have been that better
But clouds of melancholy hide the sun of
joy
Telling me you, oh my dear were her mere
toy
They mock me, ask me how could I fall in
love
When it was never my destiny
My face goes red, I know no answer
They keep on with their crass banter
I take it up all on me with sheer silence
Till the time they slut shame your
benevolence
We may not be destined for being together
But I respect you for the love no matter
©Mayank Dhar

Innocent tears

He was the best of all, his innocence knew
Chocolates, teddies and toy cars
He brought all whenever he came
The hugs of love suddenly had changed
His arms seemed more of chains
Sweet little lips of his
Rubbed till they almost bled
Glowing blue eyes ready to cry
His Words almost dry
No..His breath could only manage
The little mind puzzling with this;
Why was uncle behaving so strange
Why were his hands in my zippers
Don't do this it feels real bad
No one loves me like this
Every time mom says u will come
Every time dad plans a drink with you
I dread what are you going to do
I hate even chocolates now
Don't like to play in class
Mom and dad I want to tell u this
Please don't bring monster uncle home
I can't study as i see his face in books
It's hard to tell u all
Please understand what's troubling my
heart
©Mayank Dhar

Meenu Agarwal

Meenu Agarwal , Born On 31st Dec. At Bhiwadi, District : Alwar, Rajasthan. Currently she is pursuing MBA (Finance). She is student as well as a writer. She writes Poetry, Articles, Stories and Shayari. She is well mannered and positive person who loves and admire family values. She has amazing writing skill that touches everyone's heart.

My Love

My Love
I feel Lost in your Arms,
No Worry and no Harms,

A Beautiful Desire! To be yours,
Like Rain's drops are Clear and Pure,

Our Relation is based on Trust,
You are my Love like Desert of Thrust....
©Meenuagg

Rose Diamond

Yes! I have a lot of 'Scars',
My life is full of wounds,
A struggle continue in my mind,
My heart reflects different Sound...

A lazy person with negative thoughts,
No hope and no desires,
But when I met you under the sun rays,
I feel inside a powerful fire...

You change me and my life,
A golden dream I saw with open eyes,
My wish of rainbow has come true,
I found a 'Rose Diamond' in YOU...!!
©Meenuagg

Merlin Priyadharshini

Merlin Priyadharshini is an aspiring poet. She was born and raised in a small town of Tamil Nadu. She is currently based in Bangalore after her wedding. She has completed Electrical Engineering from the Anna University. She is a blogger and freelance editor. She had always been a poetry lover and began writing poetry at her early teens. She likes melodies and also accompanies herself in the church choir.

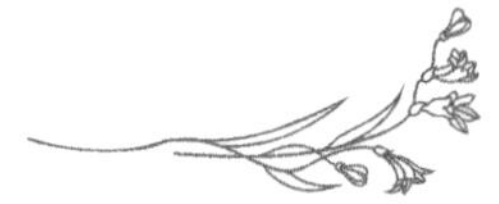

The bride

She walks up the aisle
As the bell rings from the steeple,
Decked with fragrant roses,
Their scent infiltrating every senses.
She wears a dazzling white frock,
With a veil flowing from her goldilock,
A diamond necklace around her neck;
Her elegance makes each one peck.
Her pink lips and her smoky eye
Intoxicates senses like rye.
She walks holding her father's hand,
Ready to wear the wedding band,
With a bouquet of roses;
To answer the chaplain's poses.
Musicians play the 'Bridal March' symphony
To greet the angelic bonnie.
The choir sings, "I vow to thee -
My Country," as she glows with glee.
Her cheeks are rosy, flustering,
Her eyes in joy are glittering.
She walks up to her love,
To make the eternal vow.
As the clock chimes,
She wakes up rime;
Thinking of her dream,
Her eyes radiating leam.
She rings up her man
To tell of her sweven.
©Merlin Priyadharshini

An aspect of the divine

A million folds on her primitive face;
Each of her hair light and pearly;
Her green eyes gauzy and transpicuous;
She yielded a glance delicately.

From a single peek of her,
Percolated a myriad of words;
Unuttered, yet full of tenor;
Profound, fervid, deep and intense.

She stooped as she traipsed,
Because of her hunched spine.
She paused for a while and glimpsed,
And delivered me an innocent grin.

I stayed immobile where I stood,
As her smile pervaded into my heart.
It was something, rich, rare and unrivaled;
A smile I never bumped into in my past.

She held her hand out asking mine,
I stretched out my palm as response.
She clasped it, uttering locution;
And blessed me holding tightly my manus.

I remained all agog astonishedly.
For there teemed a hundred humanity,
Who came to that church routinely.
However, she didn't bless anyone, but me.

Why did she beatify me?

A girl she neither came across;
The one she never talked to ante;
I resemble her daughter or grand girl,
perhaps.

Or did she listen to my prayers?
Is she psychic or abstruse?
Can she behear my soul of souls?
Is she bestowing me my wishes?

Nonetheless, I have never happened on
Such a woman, amicable and warm-
hearted.
She consecrated me and trailed from the
shrine;
I stared at her till she petered out from my
sight.

I felt like seeing God in her pretense,
Came down to the earth to bequeath me a
reward.
For there had been none for me all these
days,
And I had put all my trust on the almighty
God.
©Merlin Priyadharshini

Tread softly on the wings of prayer

To experience serenity's air

 in the Psithurism of the trees...

and know that peace is

most likely to be there

©Jeanette Dsouza

Monica Agarwal

Monica Agarwal born on19th June at Moradabad UttarPradesh, India did her Masters in Organic Chemistry.
She is a Chemistry Teacher. She is passionate about gardening, cooking, embroidery, reading, and loves traveling.
She is writing poems since a decade and her poems are mostly based on emotions and based on current affairs.

Mother earth

Ah!, Alas thy heard at the mid of the night,
When the sun has winded its bright light,
I ran here and there to know who was
moaning;
And found it to be my neighbour, the Earth,
who was groaning;
I comforted her on my shoulder,
And asked, dear what makes you sad and
alas;
She kept on weeping without a word,
Then with a cold sigh she put forward;

It's my children, who hurt me a lot,
They are making my life hell and rot;

They are polluting rivers which are my
blood,
Even do not realise it causes flood;

They dig my chest without taking rest,
But still I give space for their souls to rest;

They cut the trees, which purify my air,
And fill the atmosphere with polluting
layers;

But now they are testing my patience,
They want to leave me in search of better
destinations;

They want to go to you MARS,

And hope you will welcome them with open
arms;

I too wish they find happiness at least there,
And do not betray you as they have done
here;

Being a mother, I shall only give,
Till my last breathe
And
Let them long live
And
Let them long live
©Monica Agarwal

Being a girl

Being a girl is not a fun
Even though I am second to none

They try to kill me before I am born
But eventually if born, am hastily drown

I have to play with dolls and kitchen set
As I am not allowed to practice at net

People stare at me, even at the age of three
Yes, I am too young, but still not free

I'm harassed in every possible way they can,
Not safe even in school bus or van;

As I enter my teens, life changes drastically
I am abandoned from all joys in life

tragically;

Life as a young girl is not at all charming
Sometimes even my father's footsteps are
alarming

They touch me, wherever they want '
Even in dreams, they come and haunt;

Guidelines are given for do's and don'ts,
Even then each passer by passes a taunt;

At the age of 18, I am married
One house to another like cattle, I am
carried;

Here's everyone wish I have to take as a
command,
Else am threatened to be taken to remand;

I have to work from dawn to dusk,
Washing, sweeping, cleaning and collecting
the husk;

Working whole day becomes absolutely
fine'
Believe or not I do not have a minute of
mine;

From morning 5 to evening 9
From breakfast, through lunch, till everyone
dine;

News of your conception was broken to me,
Not a girl I prayed to thee,

It was not that I did not want her to be

But I could not see her suffer like me;

Thus, I prayed to thee,
She shall not be
She shall not be
©Monica Agarwal

Nidhi Sehgal

Nidhi Sehgal , a writer, poetess, reviewer and an editor, is a devoted mom. She is brought up in a small town of Uttar Pradesh and now enjoying her marital life, in the city of one of the seven wonders i.e. Agra. Nivita is her first solo collection of Hindi poems. For her, writing is her passion and everlasting dream.
You can get in touch with her at:-
Facebook:-http://www.facebook.com/nidhee.sehgal
Instagram:-@feelingsbywords__

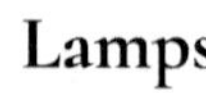

Lamps

If lamps could speak,
They gently urged the night
To stay a little longer;
As the frigid breeze of winds were still
effecting the flames of the lamps
And they are dancing bright.
Looking at the deserted paths to direct
strangers,
Giving them the beams of their own sight.

If lamps could speak,
They sang serenade for the moon,
Which peeked out of the window of clouds,
Blushingly accepting the love tune,
Magnificently they both blend into
eachother
On the starry covered lagoon.

If lamps could speak,
I used to hear the fairy tales from them,
Felt the warmth and coziness of their flame,
Slept on their motherly bosom.
©Nidhi Sehgal

My small nostalgic casket

While cleaning my bygone small casket,
My eyes stuck to the memories filled
basket,
Some monochrome pictures and some are
full of vibrant hues,
All have evoked the souvenir of my buoyant
schmooze ,
The freaky naughtiness of the age of
juvenile,
All begin running unconsciously in the veins
of nostalgic tunnel,
That, frolic summer noons,
And the playful monsoons,
That nithered cozy winters,
that were spent near bonfires,
That, pettish anger for a while
And then got united with lots of smiles,
All together brings a reminiscent of my
lovely adolescence ,
Fragrance of that mesmerising memories
are renewing the puberty with adherence.
©Nidhi Sehgal

Nirupama Jayaram

Nirupama Jayaram, she writes in the pen name of njram6. She is from the capital city of Tamil Nadu. Being an arts graduate, cooking and craft work are her hobbies lately she fell in love with words which made her to write poems. Quenching her poetic thirst by inking and reading, she contributed her works in several anthologies, often participates in writing competition in social media. Writing is not mere a hobby but a passion to her!

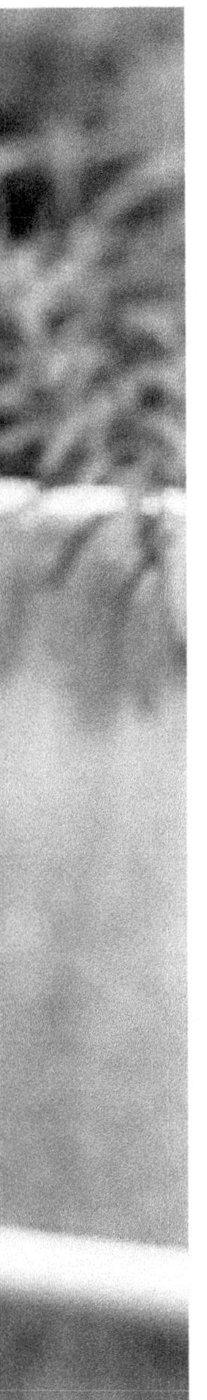

Wanton desire

Paradelle Poetry Form

Oh my darling try to soak our soul, let's rule
Oh my darling try to soak our soul, let's rule
Eradicate our haunted phlegm
Eradicate our haunted phlegm
Oh my! Our soul haunted
Soak our phlegm darling, try to eradicate it,
let's rule

The throes of humdrum chasing our
shadows
The throes of humdrum chasing our
shadows
Soul Consume wanton desire, pyre our old
enemy to ashes
Soul consumes wanton desire, pyre our old
enemy to ashes
Our shadows pyre our old enemy, the
humdrum
Ashes chasing the throes of soul to
consume wanton desire.

Kissing every bit mended our missing feel
Kissing every bit mended our missing feel
We felt the warmth of the blazing campfire
We felt the warmth of the blazing campfire
The blazing campfire mended our missing
feel
The warmth of kissing we felt every bit

The shadows of our old enemy chasing our
soul
The blazing phlegm eradicate the humdrum
The throes of haunted soul mended, pyre
to ashes
Try to soak every bit of our missing feel
Kissing, we felt the warmth of the campfire
Oh my darling! Consume wanton desire let's
rule it.
©njram6

Silent waves
Trenta-Sei Poem Form

Flavouring the feel of love in me
Let me undress the fear of loneliness
Silently listening, waves in heart's sea
I dissolve myself in happiness
Thy feel unlocked the ribs silently
I submit myself to it happily

Let me undress the fear of loneliness
Lining each moment with peace
Reverie, laughter opiates, fate's kindness
Oh! Love spirit of mine awaits for thee to
cease
Dousing in its pristine hue and flow
Surprised by its stain and glow

Silently listening, waves in heart's sea
Gracefully washed all anger, once I had
Hold me tight, let's explore shades of love
in glee
Until we attain ecstasy and evade

Embracing thee felt an unique courage
At this moment feel of mine, divulge

I dissolve myself in happiness
Unfurling love in me, bid adieu are those
revulsion
Love fire kindled, blazing in its richness
Filling the gaps with its possession
Oh my love! Freedom and love go together
This life of mine with love is smoother

Thy feel unlocked the ribs silently
Heard rhythm from the delicate den
My feel soubresaut elegantly
Symbolising our first love, lilacs bloom
again
Akin to the magenta lilacs I blush
Legs piroutted in madness, painting its lush

I submit myself to it happily
Love! Come together we dwell in city of love
Streets of Venice talk our story officially
The nelipot tread slowly, to write saga of
above
Let's satiate this marvelous passion
Rhapsodising our life in its fusion.
©njram6

Mooning moon is alluring,

Stars gazing from clutter.

Bejeweled stream radiating,

Intoxicated heart flutter.

Psithurism's defiant humming,

Leaves quiver & zephyr ablaze.

Oaks and spruces cheering,

Galaxy stunned and amazed.

©Kumar Ramesh

Pallavi Partani

Pallavi Partani, born on 15th June, in Maharashtra Yavatmal. She is M.Tech in Electronics and Telecommunication. She is now an enthusiastic mother of two angels. She writes poetry and essay. She belives in living life to fullest expressing herself through her writings and paintings.

Conservative kitchen

She worked day and night
to make her career bright..
not even a single boyfriend
nor partying with guys..
just to clear each and every concept
many nights she didn't slept..
she was a star of every professor
all wanted her as their mentor..
now being trolled for how she dressed
or not covering her head..
she is now busy pleasing all
trying to be everywhere without a call..

Just wanted to ask is this what she deserved
!!
just wanted to be safe with so called home
politics !!
just wanted to let her mind be calm peace
and blissful..
with no ifs' and buts'..
© Pallavi Partani

Life

What is life !!
life is my dad's hug
life is my mom's kiss
life is pampering my little sister..

Amidst the game of bow and arrow
when life stretches back me tight
spark in my Dad's eyes shows me focus
right..

Playing the life's snakes and ladder
my Mom's smile fixes all the hardest
teaches to live each moment to its fullest..

Seesaw highlights the ups and downs
all that tickles in the tummy around
listening my little sisters laughter to every
steps around..

My life my family
makes me to paint the life I love to poster
filling it with all the colors of Roller Coaster..
©Pallavi Partani

Dr Pragya Suman

Dr Pragya Suman, is a doctor by profession, and she is posted in shri Krishna medical college, Bihar ,India. Writing is her passion which she inherited from her father. Her father Late Triveni Prasad yadav was a civil engineer.

a

My Father's Wristwatch
Prose Poetry Form

A white wrist watch was left alive in my
father's ash urn. I wrapped it in my tiny
hand. I grew up vertical
and the watch also became a rounded one,
in a wall clock. Nowadays it hangs on the
wall beside my father's portrait.
I am stick of minute, moving round in.
One day two shooting stars dropped upon
it, and the wall clock fell down on the floor.
My tiny wrist broke down in a mangled
minute of stick. My mother told me not to
fix, otherwise my fingers would break also.
Stick of hour has gone thousand times
round, though my minutes are stagnant,
still. My mother lives in my broken minute
stick.
I am still trying to fix it with my mother's
knife!
©Dr Pragya Suman

The Potato Eaters

Vincent dipped his figurative fingers
in the earthen bowl ,
was sodden in sweat for years .
Potatoes were stuffed in
sunken cheeks, bulge eyes were sipping
the black tea .
In canopy of pale bulb
The Netherlands was dark and dark!
Painter picked a single wrinkle,
and nudged his star
Vincent's ear are still stuck,
in bowels of,
The Potato Eaters!
©Dr Pragya Suman

Prerna Anmol

She belongs to Chapra, a small town in Bihar and pursued Post Graduation in English Literature from Banaras Hindu University, Varanasi. To her, writing is life and river is idol. She believes in a life that flows like a river which never stops. Art is her passion. Spreading love, smiles and happiness is the aim of her life. Through inking, she takes shapes in various Hindi anthologies. Her Sea is far ahead. She is a learner expanding horizons and sailing her voyage without concerning about the destination.

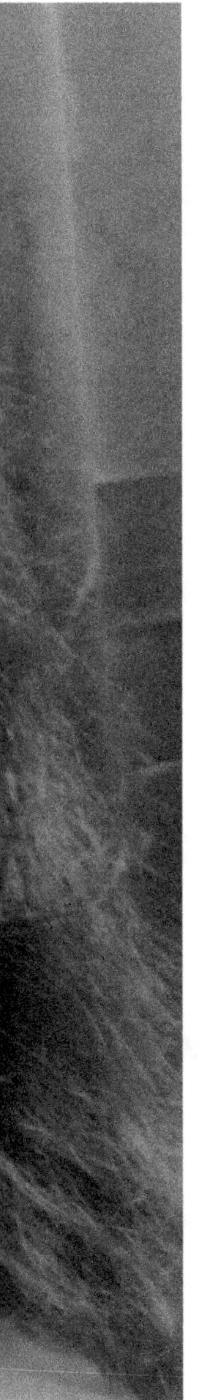

I adore imperfections

I love wandering,
In ocean of thoughts,
Sometimes good,
But wicked ones too,
So, where do you find me?
Amidst those scary sores?
No, never
You can snap me
here in my words
I'm an amiss maiden,
Like an error on a card
Or, a tremorous voice,
Singing the romantic songs
My mind is a ditch of catch-22
I may be a sweet poison,
Whom you want to be
Every time with you
I'm not the one who unwrap you
But that ghastly sole to whom
You want to surrender yours all
I am also not like
A touch of bow of Cupid,
But I can tear your heart,
Without any arrow
You can find me in silent waves
Which you have never seen
You can also search me here
In melody of buried
but lively beams
You will be in love,
If you will ever know me,

But I'm that weirdo
Who can make the hell
Of your heavenly wills
I'm that Midas
Whose touch
makes you priceless
And lastly left you alone
With me,
You will live while dying
Without me,
You will smile while crying
Listen to me again,
Never try to find me in excellence
Whenever you see,
the flaws within beauty
I'll be there
Because I adore imperfections
©Prerna Anmol

Mathematical Illusion

I add some virtues,
And subtract the vices
Multiply my illimitable love,
But forget to divide.
In my dreams too,
You are under perimeter
And I never find out
Any proofs, why,
Why I always treat you
As a radius, and not a diameter?
I am a separate zero,
And you are an individual nil
But together we can

Touch the circumference of infinity
Then why,
Why I always create an equilibrium,
In my fancies too?
I wish this arithmetic adjective
Will be vanished soon,
And I can create an honest illusion
The world of I and you.
©Prerna Anmol

Sound Of Breath

Dwelling in abyss

Psithurism

Over Dried leaves

Of Desires

@birajv

Pushpalatha Ramakrisnan

Pushpalatha Ramakrisnan is the Associate professor of English who had worked at various govt. colleges at Tamil Nadu. She is more inclined towards spirituality and has been doing meditation since early age. So far has published books relating to the Inward journey. Her book The Reverie subtitled as The Inward Journey is full of soulful songs feeling with the quest of god in to the innermost recess of human heart. She had prepared course materials for all English literature students ranging from UG to PG and prepared translations for other Humanity subjects too. Knowing self is Success is also the most remarkable of her contribution. The other translation on The Yoga Vedam is soon to be released about the Mahaguru Babaji Maharaj.

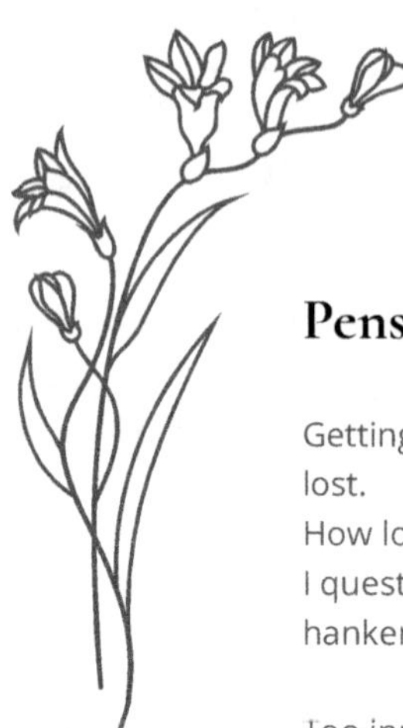

Pensive Mood

Getting into the wilderness of thought I was
lost.
How long I remained still seemed a mystery
I questioned myself why I was in a rat race
hankering after fame, name

Too innocent to know the ways of the
world.
Ma used to say that I could nt survive
in this world, often looking at my candid
nature

Whatever she feared never happened
A nice job at the age of a fresher
Being loved by all for the sweetness
of temper, the readiness to take any
challenge, never hating any even the wrong
was done.
Too much of responsibilities, doing with a
style of my own
having met with accidents 18 times
not a single injury was inflicted

I am the good child of God under the
ambience of His infinite grace
Feeling to be always at his close proximity

I wondered at every phase of my life
Feeling now about the extra
Sensory perception
I need to say many things

Sometimes I feel slighted
humiliated why it happens so
still remains a puzzle
Ye men and women I may rather go
to the house top and harangue

I am a lover of Mankind
for I see all but the manifestations of
Almighty
I see everything with ease
for my lord will lift me against the current
of life like a leaf.
© Pushpalatha Ramakrisnan

Quarantine

Far from the madding crowd
sitting in my room ruminating the ills
all are subject all over the parts of the
world.
Who will come to the rescue of all?
Will it come to an end?
Very deserted lanes
Sad to see unfrequented roads
No laughter of kids moving with glee

in around spread
Ensconced by everything seen and heard

Feeling like a sandwich between the inlaws

putting up with everything

like a tin fitted with a lid
whiling time with intellectual speculations
Yet hope lingers in me
Waiting for better prospects
To set the wheel in motion.
© Pushpalatha Ramakrisnan

Hummingbirds gather

To harvest a moist flower

They are too many

Like moths to the killing flame

The beauty bigger than life.

©Ayo gutierrez

Ramesh Kumar KG

Ramesh Kumar KG writes with pen name Kumar Ramesh. Born on 21 May 1953, is a veteran from Indian Armed Forces where he served for 38 years. Post retirement he had a short stint in banking industry. He is a native of Kerala but had his schooling in central India. Reading has been very close to his life. Writing is recently adopted offshoot of it. Love for languages is deep rooted in his thoughts and expressions. Post retirement he has finally settled down in his home town in Kerala.

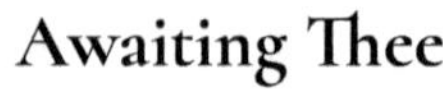

Awaiting Thee

Lengthy curvy trough of rose beds ember,
Fragrance being carried by sleepy breeze,
Mooning moon peeps, behind cloudy
chamber.

Exotic splendor blue, makes my heart
freeze,
Speechless swoon of joy, robs my heart's
treasure,
Bucolic beau alcove, sate heart to please.

I moan and move to zenith of pleasure,
Dazzling cobalt cool milieu, consume me,
Cascading passion engulfing azure.

Lane of heart you saunter, awaiting thee,
Eagerly flutters , nearness swollen heart,
Effulgent surround, tossing turning me.

Keen to mingle souls, waft to never part,
Entwined will be frames, grimly now apart.
©Kumar Ramesh

Solitude, Me & Ocean

When anxiety grips my lonely heart,
How can I not love you even more?
When solitude is all to be thwarted,
Foaming warm wave, my only anchor.
Mortified is jilted love and so it's fury,
Liquid mirror lave, soothing my hate.
Desolate heart's and seeping injuries,
You mammoth sea, savior of my state.
While rising & seeking sky, wave tips,
Kisses leave imprints, on my hurt lips.
Loose sand under feet, your silver heel,
Mighty your embrace, pearly look & feel.
Moon in bursting bloom, attempting kiss,
Night winds soar, you chase in frock blue.
Worries & melancholy, sunk in deep abyss,
Feel alone yet I do, aren't you a loner too?
©Kumar Ramesh

Ranjana Bansal

Ranjana Bansal (jazbat) has a great passion for writing which for her is a finest source to express her feelings through different forms of creation poetry, article, short stories etc.
She is professionally a school Principal and working in education field since last 24 years.
Her poetry has been published in 2 anthologies earlier also and she has been awarded with certificates of appreciation by different sites online for her writings.

Move on

Men may come and men may go
But I go on forever....

Life is a perennial stream
knows not to stop ever
Days will happen so as night
It's an unchangeable pattern
Birth is certainly followed by death
Generations revises who cares
Sun will set and definitely will shine
dusk and dawn will surely combine
So don't lose heart, play your part
Life has for all, a fixed chart
So cheer up, join the pace
If can't win, at least don't miss the race...
because
Men are mortal... Life is immortal...
It goes on and on and on for ever.
©jazbat

Life - a boon

So tender soft innocent infant
I opened my eyes,
Life had gripped me,
so I was called alive.
I was warned to be so cautious
in dealing with it or would lose it...
For me it is a gift to cherish,
same time a challenge to accept!
It has awarded me with relationships
attention respect & achievements
It is a onetime offer
never know rather believe
if I would get it again
For that don't want...
any stone unturned remain!
I speak to it when sit alone
recall with it the days gone
It consoles with full passion
Ignoring it's worth is today's fashion.
I collaborate the way it comes
Knowing ultimately I shall turn fumes.
©jazbat

Riya Bansal

Riya Bansal, born on 2nd May,1982 at Pilibanga
(Rajasthan), did her Masters in Arts and B. Ed.
She works as Lecturer of Economics at a govt. school
from last 15 years in Rajasthan. She is fond of writing
English poems as free verse and Hindi poems as free
verse, Nazm, Haik, choka, taanka, triveni and stories.
She loves to visit different states of India, and
exploring the beauty of their tourist places and
wants to know about their culture and traditions.a

My Heart

My heart weaves life
with the threads of
Feelings, likes, dislikes
Aspirations, dreams and desires
I love to feel its beat
in its joy in victory, in its efforts
In its disappointments in defeats
And yes........also in its silliness
All of these is reflected in me
As a Sparkle
The day...there will be
No thread of hope left
The day...it will stop making me
Feel its presence
I will be alive but Lifeless...
©riya Bansal

Innocence

Oh innocence!!
Why so shocked
If it didn't make any sense
So this is life
Shows you different colours
But at different price
Let everything flow
Don't try to hold tight
Believe me sweetheart...
You are fairy queen of your sky
Trust your wings
But never leave ground
To fly so high
Go ahead with your inner spark
Why to stop to find answer of any silly "why"
Itself will come looking for you one day
And I am damn sure
You'll need no answer that day...
©riya Bansal

Rose George

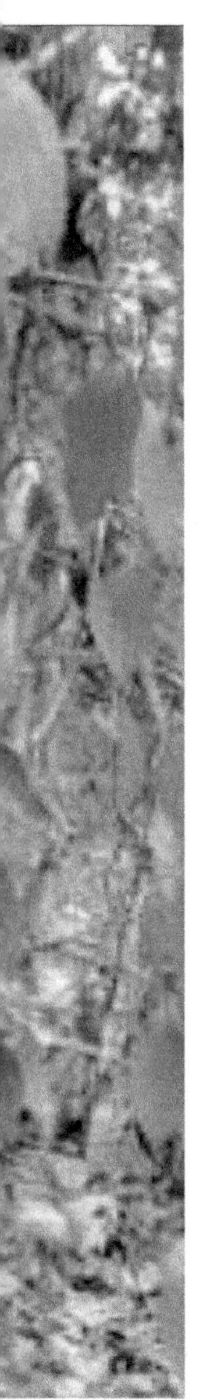

Rose George from Kerala completed her post graduation from the University of Mumbai. She has been teaching in the Junior College for the last 25 years. Her passion is writing. She has written poems for many anthologies. She has contributed in the publications of various school magazines, newsletters. She has organised language fests and contributed to various literary activities.

Petrichor

O! the parched longing of the earth
Welcoming with joy the blissful rain
Drizzling drops so heavenly
Smell of the mild petrichor
Lingering and tickling my nostrils
Aroma so refreshing and invigorating
Beauty of nature so enchanting
Silver liquid drops glistening on the leaves
Branches swaying in delight
The petrichor emanating on the green grass
Magic in the air all around
Inhaling the warmth of the petrichor
So soothing and uplifting
My soul rejuvenating with joy
As it satiates and quenches my thirst
O! the smell of the petrichor, so eternal and
divine
©Rose George

Fleeting Flora

O! what beauty lies in the floral blooms
In the green meadows and the vast
landscapes
Mountains and forests, so enthralling
Diversity of the plant species breathtaking

O! we rested in the lap of nature
Feeling so relaxed and peaceful
Beautiful flowers exuding their sweet
fragrance
Medicines fruits and food, the precious gifts
of flora

Alas! the flora is fleeting with time
Global warming and climatic changes
Deforestation and landscape development
Affecting the flora and fauna

Come on, let us save the flora from fleeting
Giving up our selfish interests and greed
Stop it from harm through exploration and
scientific inventions
Giving back to her, just as she has served us
with love
©Rose George

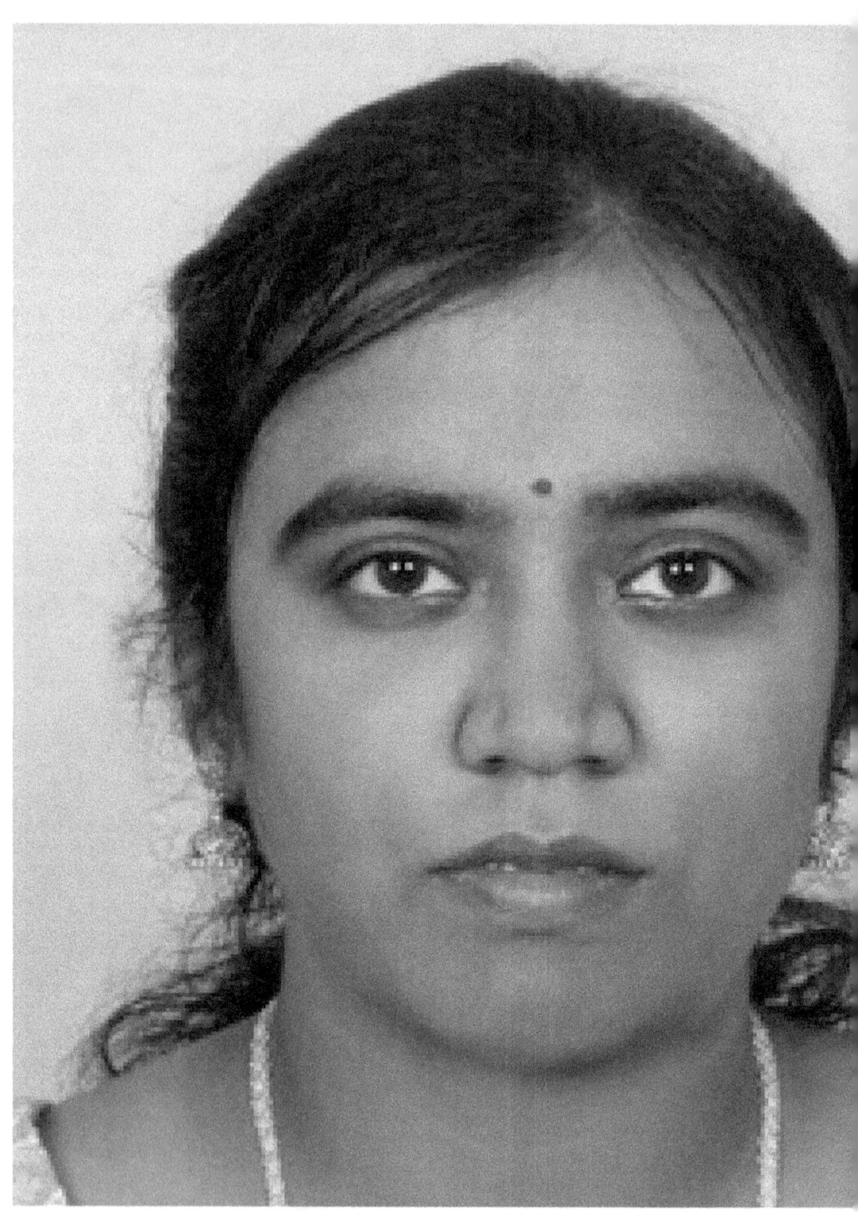

S Gayathri Vijayaragavan

S GayathriVijayaragavan born on 4th October 1992 in Tamilnadu. Gayathri did B.E in 2014 and M.E in 2016 . Gayathri is an engineer. Her writing style is poetic and lyrical. Her enthusiasm, willingness to learn and experiment gave the push for an amusing, enthralling and flabbergasted journey to start every day.

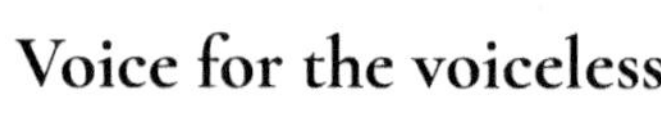

Voice for the voiceless

Once existence defines the subsistence.
Illuminating the obscure memories.
Thriving the intriguing distance.

Lurking each sceneries
Swishing maunder vision.
Striving amusing theories.

Certain interval fissures mission.
Strangling the unwarranted thought.
Paving the unknown tension.

Still my mind get caught.
Reverie the unsorted dream.
Weaving the fascinating stories to sought.

Reverberating the narration to flow as
stream.
Searching the voice for the voiceless in
every scream. ©kosachaya

Dew of hope

Shredded pieces diffuse the cohesive art.
Rumbling the rhythm to glide.
Threaded sheath provide voluptuous start.

Quilling the verses with humungous tide.
Though the perspective varies.
Resonating life with every ride.

Mind bewilder the triggered memories.
Lacing the withered past.
Time adhere the undisputed libraries.

Dwindling the permeate cast.
Letters create occluded emotion.
Shimmering the obscure traces to be
passed.

Writings delineate the gigantic notion.
Where dew of hope enshrine with various
motion.
©kosachaya

Sandeep Kumar

A giant dreamer and agnostic individual. He
is someone who lives by words even after
understanding the pains of it and is a rebel in today's
world. By profession a banker who still believes in
taking up his responsibilities even without being
assigned but can't help it. Uses a pen name of
Zindadilsandeep as he believes everything shall
pass someday be it good or the bad, but the outlook
always decides the person we become. On Instagram
@zindadilsandeep
Has a website www. Kuchehsaasankahese.com
which is awaiting writers and artists to lead the way
for smiles amidst the tears and rush of life.

Immigration - a conversation with life

There I was looking for the stars.
All around me now is the fear of scars.
Closed by the walls silently we live.
Spontaneous pain is what we always give.
Millions stranded on stations waiting for a train.
where to live? where to die? asks the human brain.
I was there when greed was not a essentiality.
I was there when nature was full of flair.
Noone assumed these days are so near.
Myself life, standing by you have no fear.
Don't be slaves bounded by chains.
Love thy all share the grains.
This too shall with a lesson learnt along.
BE MORE HUMANE NOT RIGHT OR WRONG.
©Zindadilsandeep

Naked truth

Insight of the soul wandering along the
time.
no feelings so pure when innocence
becomes a crime.
joys and glory subdued and limited to few.
hungry stomach, eyes full of tears no more
are new.
walking miles when life becomes a misery.
human so selfish running for a treasury.
we were the ones who build your home.
now u refuse us leaving all alone to roam.
appetite becomes a question when we
walk.
born in the slums, we die in the dark.
once and for all take all you can.
god created humans, devilish are the plan.
say it all when life's gonna be a scared walk.
everyone will have to pay pride will watch
in gawk.
©Zindadilsandeep

Saraswati Poswal

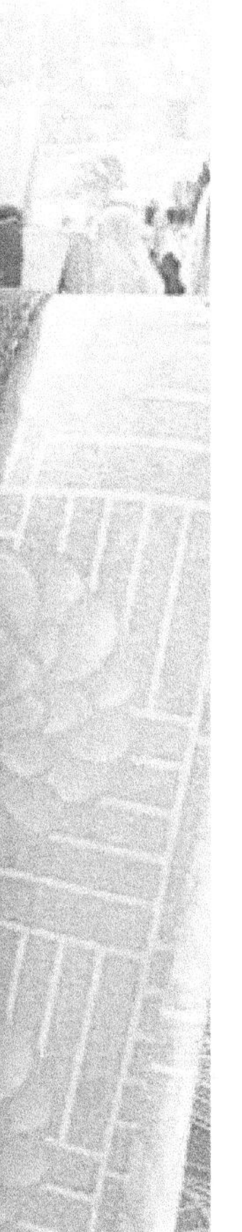

About the Poetess Saraswati Poswal has penchant for writing poems. She is writing for many literary groups. She has written many poems for many prompts and segments. Many of her poems are published in many Anthologies. She is author at her book 'Musing Showers' which was released by Anand Neelkantan Writer of 'Rise of Gajgamini'. She is working as editor for many Anthologies. She writes in English, Hindi and Punjabi. One of her Punjabi Poem is published in Amravati Prisma which awarded for Limca book of records 2016. Her poem 'Story of a Liberal Women' was selected among top three all over the world in Parnasso Italy. She has done up with more than 40 books India and around the World. Poetry on life, Nature and Society.

Shades of life

Life carries the distinct shades with
perceptions of distinct minds.
Various colours of flowers bloom.
Sometimes only dark and sometimes
glooms.
Some are faded and dusky brooms.
Some days are vibrant like the violet hues
Some are milky white...
Bestowing peace in you.
Some are green like hues.
Some are golden like the rays of sun.
Crunchy and adorned.
Some leave the silver effects.
Grey shades for some.
Some are redeemed like the rose.
Some blush in pink and pose.
Perceptions, "What we adore".
Those shades we wore.
Some times nights are chosen to be bright
Some times days become the beckoning
dark like night.
This is norm of every life.
©Saraswati Poswal

Twist of nature

Twist of Nature
Nature turned around
Being soundless
Witness of truth
Cure for The whole
Mankind.
Continuous pollution
Which was draining out
And motionless sounds
Surrender selflessly
Like the river
Carrying the spectrum
Of light
Humans purging
Trees.
For the use of materialistic life.
When whole mankind
will demolish
then learn to make
the nature survive.
Breath is essential
For sapling or leaves
Let them live
Untouched
Unspoken
Simply listening
To their
Whimsical sounds
And enhancing
With enduring
And not spreading

Pollution for saving
Their life...
And nature will save
the whole mankind..!!
©Saraswati Poswal

The birds warbled and the trees fiddled

The breeze sang and all of nature rang A harmonious flow of

esthetic row

Tis the irenic divinism of psithurism

@tega_benny

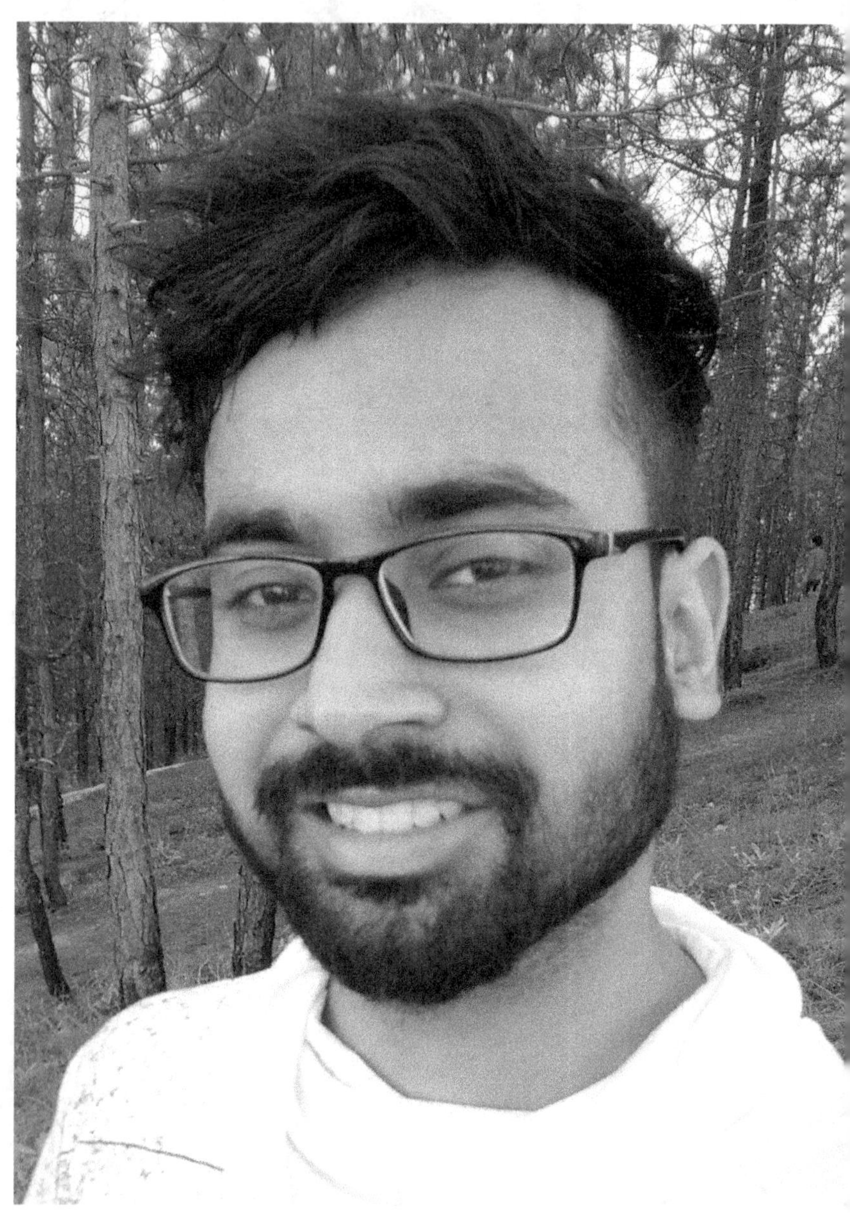

Sarthak Chamoli

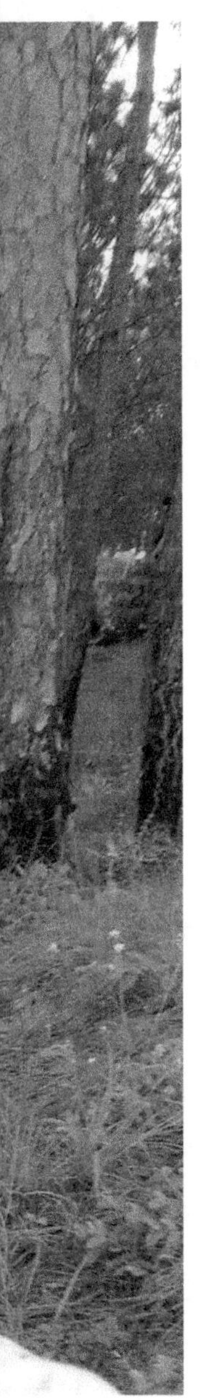

Hailing from Uttarakhand , Sarthak pursues a degree in civil engineering but has an insatiable appetite for literature. Additionally , his pen has been sprouting words recently. An observant who finds love in those little of things. He fills his soul with fitness , singing , photography and caring for mother nature. Adopt a plant and you can befriend him for life.

Three green chilies

Under the shadows of the big brown house,
a mud-house kitchen lay hidden,
Nobody dares to enter it but the old lady
and her young little friend,
The midget rests peacefully on the bed of
mint leaves and the green chilies,
And when the old lady wants she would ask
her for some green chilies daily,
Little girl's eyes never fail, as she picks and
serves the old lady, the chilies and mint that
prevail,
Enter they through the door, with legs
crossed they sit on the earthen floor.

The little girl wonders how the old lady bent
as a bow lifts the heavy grinding stone?
She grinds and grinds the leaves with all the
strength her body knows, forgetting all the
pain she keeps in her skin and bones,
Stops and ponders, she wonders then dips
a finger in the paste,
Nods and nods and nods and disgraces the
taste,
Looking at her little friend she pleaded
"Three green chilies is all that is needed"
The little girl's little feet in fleet in the fuss,
hair flying in the muss she rush and hush,
Bent on knees she plucks the leaves in the
same routine,
On her back she clings and swings and
flings the chilies on her lap,

Old lady looks at her and claps,
She grinds and grinds, and grinds again,
Until the paste she attains,
Dips her finger and smiles now with no
distrain.

They did the same for days and weeks
Till one heavy morning when the sky was
bleak.
The old lady was in her room,
Her hand was holding a big broom,
Her deaf ears could hear all queer and saw
a group of men standing near
And her eyes didn't cheer.
In worst of all her fears,
They filled the mud house with the cement
grouts,
And in the loud sound , she shouts
But all was in vain, they did not see the
pain,
She went to bed, not turning her head,
Lied there she all alone,
Watching die her golden throne.

When the little girl comes to meet,
Her eyes still in glee
She couldn't see the old woman's flee
How her old cold body leaves the soul
And wanders around but the mud house it
couldn't explore
Lies her body dead on the ground
Her dried lips could no more make a sound
But the little girl stands confused and
throws the chillies on her lap to implore,
"Granny! Here are some chilies, or you want
three more?"
©Sarthak Chamoli

Ride

Riding with indolence in his lucid path,
With head held in the air that's keeping him
apart.
Knitting intangible clouds left in his heart,
Racing like thunder, hoping things will last.

Rain drops of diffidence falls on his
shoulder,
His burning soul strangling him, his body
smolders,
Nibbling soul, should have sold her.

Rotten leaves on the ground hiding his
shadows,
Showers in melody of dusk and moonlight,
his head held low,
Heard a rumble, stood up, it was his
indignation though.

Crawls now he with trepidation stumbling
on laughter,
Sad smile on his face who his he after?
Eyes seek light, of what he is a master
Warm breath, frozen head, his teeth clatter.

A rapacity of shelter,
No ammunition needed now,
Mud incise his body,
Vaguely vanishes vanity.
©Sarthak Chamolia

The spirit of the breeze wanders around

Endowing wistful souls with the charisma of a sound

Only a few hear it

The idyllic ones who listen for it

@tega_benny

Shabana Khan

Shabana Khan, born in Surat, Gujarat & settled in
Pune. She studied in a boarding school at Panchgani.
Her family comprises of her husband & her seven
year old son. She has completed MBA – HRM, from
Pune University. She has worked with reputed
organizations as a Branch Sales Manager & Sr. HR
Executive.
Currently, she is a visiting faculty with School of Life
& conduct online storytelling classes for kid's age
group from 4 years to 9 years old.
She enjoys writing, music, driving & teaching. She is a
happy go lucky person. Her Motto - Live & let live.

Beauty of Silence

Didn't realise the beauty of silence,
Till the thunderbolt fell upon us.
A forced action,
Leaving us at the feet of Mother Earth's
mercy.

Didn't realise the beauty of silence.
Till the storm swept us from our Illusion.
The fairy tale of life,
Leaving us in pool of emotions.

Didn't realise the beauty of silence.
Till the reality hit hard,
That, nothing is permanent.
We are slaves of dependence, worldly
pleasure and relationships.

Didn't realise the beauty of silence.
Till the fear of dying,
Knocked our door.
Shouting ' hey soul what are you looking
for?'
'When the river was calm, you were
turbulent from within & now the river has
taken it's coarse & you realise its beauty?'

Didn't realise the beauty of silence.
Till i confined myself,
To self-healing,
Profound inner soul.
To heal the wounds,

That people around overlook.

 Didn't realise the beauty of silence.
Till time of hope stopped ticking.
But only hope of self-love prevailed,
To sail through the turbulent waves of
Dependence, expectations & love.
©Shabana Khan

Women

God's beautiful creation.
A heart that's soft,
But strong, emotional and unexplainable
will power.
She can make you smile & embrace you in
her arms.
Make you feel the luckiest in the world.
She will treasure you like there's no
tomorrow.
In times of trouble,
She will hold on & fight the odds.
With no fear in her eyes.

God's beautiful creation.
Whose womb gives birth to another
heartbeat.
Nurtures the child.
The only unconditional love in the world.
Every child should remember that they owe,
Their life to her.

God's beautiful creation.
Calm as the sea and wild as the storm.

You press the wrong button,
The calm sea will turn wild.
Only love can calm her.
You should know how to make a women
feel beautiful & secured.
Remember, without her,
You are nothing.
But, a body without soul.

God's beautiful creation.
A multi-faceted creation,
Performing many roles.
With sincerity, honesty & love
So let's salute all the beautiful women,
Who make this world a beautiful place.
©Shabana Khan

The forest is calm

But if we would speed up time

We would see green fire

Boiling and strangling itself

Over and over again.

©Ayo gutierrez

Sharmila Juliet

Sharmila Juliet is from small village in Erode,
TamilNadu. By profession she is a Web Developer.
She is much interested in arts. She always like
to learn new things. Her love for writing started
in school. She has been part of some interesting
Anthology's like "The Flyleaf Tale", The Burning
Outcry : Is Candle March Enough?" by Writerstolli and
"Colour My Dreams" by Geraldine Kumar.

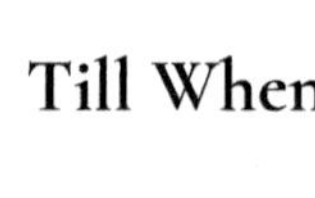

Till When

You are going to wait for a light?
When you started to walk, without
The choice scaring darkness have to
Fade away because of your brightness.
Still are you screaming out of a darkness.
Even passing lot of moonless night
Still you didn't get used to it?

Till When
You need saviour to protect yourself?
When people around you become
Prey for hungry demos masked as
Saviour everyday.
Still are you going to expect
Someone other will come to save you?

Till When
You are going to be a puppet of
Someone other's thought?
When your thoughts are capable
To flip the whole world.
Still are you going to agree with
Everything what others say
Without any objection?

Till When
You are going to wait someone else
Will come to fight for you?
When your confidence have a
Potential to create history.
Still are you not going to fight

For yourself?

Till When
You are going to depend on
Someone else?
When you have the ability to support
The society to bring new changes.
Still are you going to hide behind
Someone else?

Till when
You are going to act hopeless?
It's enough now. Raise your voice, Take
stand
Without any fear. It's the time to fight for
Yourself. Yes, It is the time for yourself
No one can defend you better than
yourself.
Let's try to be a Saviour for yourself.
Whole universe will be on your footstep.
© Sharmila Juliet

Smile

You are going to wait for a light?
When you started to walk, without
The choice scaring darkness have to
Fade away because of your brightness.
Still are you screaming out of a darkness.
Even passing lot of moonless night
Still you didn't get used to it?

Till When
You need saviour to protect yourself?
When people around you become
Prey for hungry demos masked as
Saviour everyday.
Still are you going to expect
Someone other will come to save you?

Till When
You are going to be a puppet of
Someone other's thought?
When your thoughts are capable
To flip the whole world.
Still are you going to agree with
Everything what others say
Without any objection?

Till When
You are going to wait someone else
Will come to fight for you?
When your confidence have a
Potential to create history.
Still are you not going to fight

Thickets of trees

Sprawling nonchalantly

Tranced amidst euphony

Of psithurism

@birajv

Dr.Shephali Chitre

Born in Rajasthan (India), Dr.Shephali Chitre holds double Ph.Ds in English Literature and Management Studies. She is litterateur, educationist and social thinker. She is the recipient of many awards in her profession. Dr.Shephali is a multilingual published poet and a critic. Her poetic style is free verse, personal, intimate and conversational. Her first anthology of poems, "Cognizance" was nominated for Prime Poetry Prize2019, and she was one of the highly recommended poets in it. Chennai Poet's Circle conferred Literary Award upon her for her outstanding contribution towards Poetry. Her poems are published in many national and international journals and on online poetry sites. She is a speaker, counselor and a trainer.

Drama

I sit and watch often,
gaze lively,
live drama
played daily
on stage of heart and mind
from dawn to dusk,
starring emotions
and thoughts
in lead roles.

Shocks and awes
stun the stage
giving twists and turns.
Fear, scare and terror
knock the stage with
mystery and horror.

Pains and griefs
create the emotional pangs.
Joys and happiness
create heaves of pleasure
to enjoy the stage.

Wishes and desires
boost the stage with
passion to follow the passion.
Faith and trust
decorate the stage
with garland of
confidence, dignity and pride.

I wonder,
being impartial audience
how could I create a device
to measure the immeasurable
emotional emotions,
to detect the depth
of deep thoughts,
to decide the best actor of stage -
thoughts or emotions!
©Dr.Shephali Chitre

Footprints

Walking gradually on sandy beach,
crystal gravels beneath my feet,
looking back for my traces
scanning if not swept away
with wide blue ocean.

Swaying swiftly with gentle breeze
to see visual trail of
my footprints through
rough-hewn and windy pathways
criss-crossing crossroads.

Not of stone or glass
footprints are perpetual
to feel me in grass plains
and soulful trails blowing
wind upon quiet pastures.

Tracking the bright and clear
traces of my journey

footprints tell –
the sun sets to rise, and
the wave falls to rise again,
unfolding the tale of
each passing moment.
©Dr.Shephali Chitre

Anchor & sail

Thoughts riding psithurism wail,

Seeking an anchor before its sail.

Aroma of caresses on soul prevail,

Proximity sought, but to no avail.

©Kumar Ramesh

Siddhi Chavan

Since 2 years, Siddhi Chavan ventured into Poetic world. She is fond of writing poems belonging to different types of poetry forms. She also likes to learn new words and phrases. Although she is enthusiastic about exploring new thoughts, she also enjoys to write on some challenging topics which we face in our world. Sometime back she has also written some short stories. You can find her on social media with penname Prettyproses.

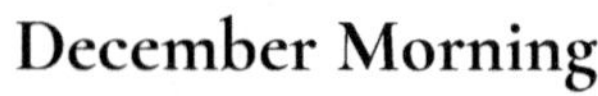

December Morning

Colours of sky pile up
And stars are still wandering
I want Winter to wake me up
On a chilly December morning

How should I decipher
What this weather is telling
Even my poetry seems so blur
Emotions from heart are escaping

I call out the lively metaphors
To suffice dead souls
Marvelled at the shining stars
Words accompany me on evening strolls

When I look up high above
This wind blowing through my face
Now I see words running from glove
Run to keep up with my thoughts pace
©prettyproses

Echoes of Spring

O floating feathers
Where have you disappeared?
When all my heart desires
Soaring in skies wings coloured

Hear what the spring echoes
In these sparkling waves of waters
Where these eyes chose
Sight of butterflies over flowers

Behold as my heart rejoices
In the fall of leaves
I have accepted climate phases
This calm serenity my mind believes

Listen to the cheerful song
Which my lips blew into cloud
When my soul is waiting since long
To hear my words breathing out loud
©prettyproses

Snigdha Gautam

From an aspiring literature student to a business student to now pursuing a Commerce degree at GGSIPU in Delhi, Snigdha's journey of varied tastes and inclinations has had her experience many colours. She has developed a liking for Finance , and plans to explore this segment more. She's unapologetically straightforward and prioritizes her values. Get her a cat and a cup of coffee and you befriend her for life

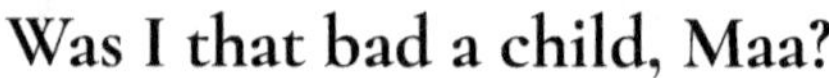

Was I that bad a child, Maa?

As I weep today to my heart's content
I ask you blatantly
Was I that bad a child, Maa?

To those thorny days
And nights unfair
As I creeped into my bed
I contemplated...
Was I that bad a child, Maa?

Your words flew like pots and pans
To my face all smeared with fresh tears...
To my efforts which seem to disappoint you
I ask you today will all guts and those tears
..
Was I that bad a child, Maa?

Was I nothing more than a reaping sack?
Was I anything more than a flunk at maths?
Couldn't you see my fleeting moment of
despair?
Was I that bad a child, Maa?

Once I was judged truly wicked
You blew down the stick on me
All fast , nothing clear.

I've a hazy memory of that day:
We burnt the midnight oil together
We did sums
I thought twas clear

As Clear as a bell
But only when you interrogated
I was found dumb with fear
My lips pursed with a blank memory
My palms sweaty on the near ghory
My eyes were all watery
Could see nothing but dark
Dark! as I envisioned my future
When YOU compared me
Dark! as I envisioned my future
When YOU couldn't understand
Dark! as I envisioned my future
When YOU gave up!

You kicked me off
I fell with a thud
Embarassment. Guilt. Fear.
Twas a concoction of these three
That very moment I gave up too
Did I long for a hug?
Did I long for consolation?
Did I long for your care?
I barely remember.

Instead, I fought my tears
Would Maa love me if I score perfect? I
wondered.
Would Maa kiss away my tears if I do
maths? I wondered.
Didn't Maa see how caring I was?
Didn't Maa notice it was fear that I had
caught?

These petty thoughts built a castle soon
Leaving me in darkness without a moon
I piled hatred and all trash in my heart

Maa, you could no longer trespass those
walls
Those walls were high and built too tough
Now I was quite all the while and didn't bluff

When I was eleven, after a beating
I took the ruler and smashed it to kindling.
Fingering the splinters I could not believe.
How could this rod prove weaker than me?
Twas not that I was never again beaten
but in destroying that stick that had
measured my pain
the next day I was an adolescent, not a
child.

This is not a tale of innocence lost but
power
gained : I would not be a mother
There's are shackles I have learnt to break.
©Snigdha

Your lines bring,

Solace to my mind.

Stirring up my thoughts,

like a gentle breeze,

flowing through,

dormant leaves;

awakening them with

psithurism of trees

@Aafiya_21

Soma Bhowmik

An Educationist and Physiological Counsellor
Specialised in : Free lancing, content writing, blog
writing, creative writing in 3 languages (English,
Hindi, Bangla), Contemporary art, Painting on canvas
and acting in short films.

Being an ambitious woman.She is attached with the
creative world as an artist and writer. As an artist her
subject is oil painting on Canvas.She is an actress.
she is an educationist running her own Montessori
school "New Era Kids".Above all she is a lady with
golden heart which gets reflected from her writings
as a poet.

Thought

In this world of terror and violence
Let's sit back and think in silence
About our wishes and real desire
Who really think and do care
Then probably we will be able to decide
our own priorities keeping everything aside.

Life is simple, life is short
Love, sympathy and empathy
Is what we have forgotten
People do care
But don't dare to share
Everyone is engrossed in their own affairs

Teach your son to respect his mom and sis
Don't teach your daughter to be selfish
Help someone in case of need
Save not on your account
but on your good deeds.

Do Forgive rather than punish
One day surely the violence will vanish.
©Soma Bhowmik

Pride

It's you ...your life
So its upon you to decide.
You will choose which direction which way
"Lady it's your day!"
You are capable
So, walk with pride
No need to pretend
Or take somebody's side
Show your attitude
You need not be always right
Cherish each and every moment in your
way
"Lady it's your day!"
Not a matter of chance
Not with an illusion
Live your life with full satisfaction
You are not a drop in the ocean
Give an example to the
World to convey
"Lady it's your day!"
©Soma Bhowmik

Ssareeta Singh

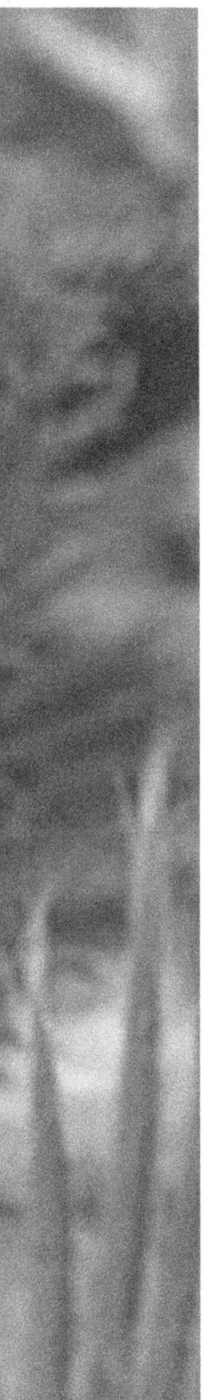

An educationist, author, social influencer and a passionate writer. Ssareeta singh is a super brain trainer and mother of three sons. She was born on 22nd march in Chandigarh. A Post graduate in English literature and pursuing PhD in same. At present she is Director of school. Her love is for free verse writing but she does try following few techniques. She is animal lover, owns an NGO and loves to work for social causes and upliftment of women.

Life

Life
The most complicated
Word
Ever known
To be understood
And mostly misunderstood
In its entirety
Nothing more
Relevant
Nothing less
Obscene
But always creating tremendous scenes
Fluctuating formations
With decent deformities
It gets ahead
As if never to be seen
But it is there always to
Remind you of truth
Make you more poignant
Unless you rule
Once you think in a certain way
It diminishes into shell
Absolutely creating a havoc and a hell
Life is a passionate poison
Waited to be engulfed in silence!
©Sherry

Betrayal

On that day my soul grew silent,
Remembering many inaudible, immobile
betrayals,
How I used to oblige even deceptive
portrayals,
The countless committal creeps,
Coming to me like faithful peace,
All that was but a illusionism,
Because they only wanted semiotic, somber
shitty stylization,
Which always bought me sweet sublime
suffering,
I was a dummy, a doll against which they
were beautifully plotting,
They carved the scheming and I came in
sneaking,
Long I stood there abducting,
Back into my memories readying,
Remembering many stoic unacknowledged
phantasms,
Never have I dreamt of such
representations,
Perfumed enigmatically from unseen
publications,
It could have been mutual revelations,
I always thought but
My absenteeism, your formalism paved a
way of flocking renovations,
Your exterior memoranda exposing,
But my heart was covered with admiring
the decorative installations,

I was shorn of my impatience,
You were but a noiseless traitor,
Many a times I tried to wake and flung to
perfidy,
But could never surpass your ornate
quiddity,
Back when myself again start installing,
I was showered with unfaithfulness and you
are a perfect filling folly,
The contretemps bought such sorrows,
The double crosser dual and detonating,
You were all this but I was ever called
melodramatic, treacherous and tagged with
various narratives,
The bugged up irresolution never saw the
end,
Every incident was intended to make me
torn apart and to never to mend,
I ever remained a tacit,
And you a periodic positioning,
Me was a deserter never versing,
With all the betrayal growing into nastiness
nearing,
I screamed with a guilt and still gentle
clinging,
My brain was astonished yet agonising,
Infact I kept for long just mumbling,
Asking everyone who keeps on coming,
Why betrayal stood upright and standing?
Whereas I was put to shame and revealing
and left unapologetically unappealing!
©Sherry

Elusive you're yet mysterious in its mystique

Nature compiled ethereal echoes

Symphony gushing and enchanting

Tread carefully in its subtle rustling

Psithurism! An immortal chasm

© njram6

Tripti Agarwal

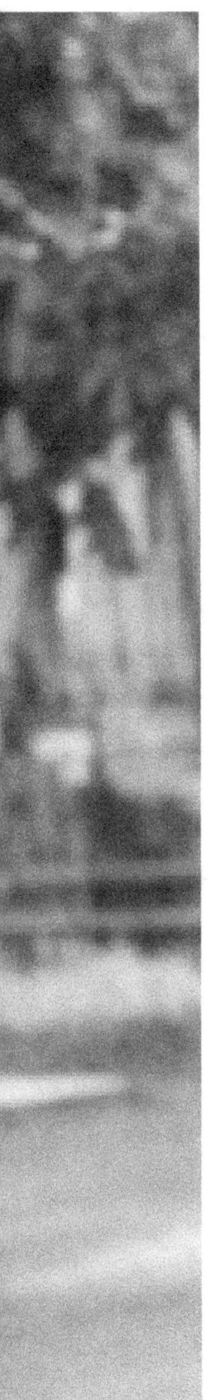

Tripti Agarwal is a Chartered Accountant by profession and pursuing Company Secretary Course. She is a small town girl with sky high dreams and have been moving across the cities in India to live by experiences. She has always been the part of Cultural and Art activities happening around her but writing came in when she learned what life is actually like, the hard way. She writes on the basis of her experiences and is always curious to gain more and give more.

Greedy Calculator

What if my calculator was me?
Greed would have engulfed
all those zeros adjacent to one.
There would have been
no million, no billion.
Just a poor zero with no mate
would survive in this filthy world.
A zero has no end
©Tripti Agarwal

My Reflection

More than mirror I see myself in other
things,
In your eyes,
My window pane,
The river outside my home,
They know me better,
All my secrets,
Since childhood I have been sharing.

When I look into your eyes,
They reflect me as epitome of love,
Which you couldn't handle,
On your weak knees.

When I look into that window pane,
I remember the rain flowing with my tears,
To dry up the pain.

When I sit beside that river bank,
It roars with me in anger,
It laughs reminding my childhood carefree
smile,
It sings those lullabies which my grandpa
used to sing for both of us.

Mirror on the wall only reflects my lip
shade,
Not the shades my soul is painted in.
©Tripti Agarwal

Vidya Vijay Chauhan

Vidya Vijay Chauhan was born in South Mumbai. Her father being a naval officer, she has led a very disciplined life. She has done her M.A in English literature, B.Ed. and MBA in school management. She is a teacher by profession but a writer with passion who expresses her thoughts on nature, women's conditions and surroundings very clearly and effectively. She is straightforward, entertaining and earnest. She believes in the ideology of devoting the God gifted life to pamper the innocent child in her and keep the goodness alive. Self-growth and physical fitness are her mantras to make everything around look beautiful. She mostly shares her emotions in free verse which is easily understood by common people.

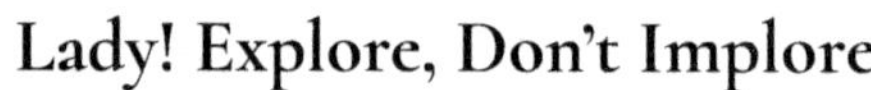

Lady! Explore, Don't Implore

Lead your own battle
Stand with your head held high
Don't follow like cattle
Albeit consequences make you sigh

Ups and downs will be a phase
Stand straight and stay strong
You don't break whoever says
Remember, difficulties won't prolong

Break the shackles
Trace your destination
Lady, only you can tackle
Stay tuned to your determination

Don't you be complaisant
Raise your voice and stay firm
How much ever they may be blatant
You live life on your terms

People who have been nefarious
Will have to pay heavy price
Have chosen way thats precarious
All in favour is your dice

Lady, you don't be docile
Make rich and high your profile

Take it all in your stride
Carve your niche, and take pride
© Vidya Vijay Chauhan

Blessings

Blessed I am
With beautiful people around
Who help me grow
Even if I am a little slow

Not only do they motivate
When my heart palpitates
They show in me complete faith
And never hesitate

Friends who are close to heart
Your feelings empower me
To enrich the art
Of which I always wanted to be a part

God! I wish to thank you
For all those gifts fantastic
That brightens up my little world
And brings me joy ecstatic.
© Vidya Vijay Chauhan

Yogita Jadhav

She belongs to the cultural city of Pune, where the company of books is rather inevitable. She possesses a degree in Law and has keen interest in aesthetics. Her hobbies include drawing and reading. She is a lover of poetry and puts her thoughts to words sometimes. Being an avid reader since childhood, writing became the natural step towards her self-expression. She believes in spreading positivity through her words and leaving behind some thoughts to ponder.

Hope

Hope watches over you and me
to see how long you hold on
When things don't seem to go
right, after the light has gone

You may not have much, but still
it's the one thing you've got
Hang on, don't just give up on
yourself, though it may seem a lot

You will tide over your failures and
rise from your ashes once again
It's just a matter of time when in
yourself, you'll faith and love regain

Some mountains may seem too
tall for your weak legs to scale
Some seas may seem too deep
to fathom, just adjust your sail

Hope is still waiting for you and me
to hold on when there's none left
Isn't it better to do what you are
good at, and hope for the best
©yogi_writes

Mother Nature

When she's happy, She'll smile...
differently everytime
She'll bloom in vibrant colours
And show up in her best green dress
She'll paint the sky with azure blue
Wear a crown of fluffy white clouds
She's coolest when she brings down the
showers
Every stream, every river, swells with
happiness
At night she'll be looking her stunning best
In a velvety black star studded dress
Smiling back at the lovers admiring her
dazzling face
Next morning, she'll rise and shine in her
resplendent self
Yes she's best, when she's happy and
smiling
©yogi_writes